LIFE OF A SCOTTISH SAILOR.

LIFE

OF A

Scottish Sailor;

OR

Forty Years' Experience of the Sea.

By JOHN BAIN,
MASTER MARINER.

NAIRN: GEORGE BAIN.

INVERNESS: MELVEN BROTHERS.   LONDON: BLISS, SANDS & CO.

CONTENTS.

	PAGE
PREFACE,	ix.-xxiii.
CHAPTER I.—INTRODUCTORY,	1
,, II.—ON BOARD A COLLIER,	8
,, III.—BEFORE THE MAST,	21
,, IV.—AS MATE,	31
,, V.—IN COMMAND,	45
,, VI.—STEAMSHIPS,	67
,, VII.—THE OCEAN HIGHWAY,	82
,, VIII.—IN THE TRANSPORT SERVICE,	92
,, IX.—ANIMALS AT SEA,	107
,, X.—MORAL IMPROVEMENT OF THE SAILOR,	120
,, XI.—CONCLUSION,	131

PREFACE.

THE writer of the following Reminiscences, Captain John Bain, well known in Glasgow as master mariner and nautical assessor, was born in 1839 and died in 1895. He was one of the most active and estimable men whom the town of Nairn has sent forth into the world. It is difficult for those who knew him well to speak of Captain Bain in language which may not seem to others to savour of exaggeration. No man was ever associated with him, no man, it may be said, ever met him, without feeling the fascination of his personal character. In manner he was unassuming and undemonstrative, but at the same time bright and genial, mentally alert and observant. He was interested in every aspect of human life, disposed to recognise what was best in his fellows, and to meet them in a spirit of friendliness and good will. A more companionable man never lived. In course of his career, from apprentice boy onwards, he associated with men of all classes and conditions, and left the same favourable impression on every person with whom he came into contact. The old fishermen at Nairn rejoiced to see him, and enjoyed a chat with him about the sea; while the most accomplished men of the world found him to be an acceptable acquaintance, well-informed, sparkling in conversation, and full of anecdote and varied experience. His attainments, which were of the most solid character, never sat heavily on him because they were enlivened by his good humour and sense of proportion. He possessed in rare measure the qualities of a cool head, a well-balanced judgment, and a warm heart. While fully versed in the ways of the world, he was singularly free from any tendency to harsh or intolerant criticism. His whole outlook on life was generous and cheerful. When the news of his premature death arrived at Nairn, every man and woman in the town felt as if a personal friend had departed.

John Bain was educated principally at the Free Church School in Nairn, at the time one of the best educational institutions in the place. He enjoyed a religious upbringing from his much respected parents, and was surrounded by the healthful and stimulating influences of a happy home. In those days boys had to begin work early, and John, who was quick-witted and well advanced for his years, entered an office at the age of eleven. His employer was inspector of poor and collector of rates, and his young assistant was entrusted with the duty of serving the notifications and obtaining the money. His experiences are touched upon in the introductory pages of his autobiography. Even at that time the boy's heart was set on the sea. He had no relative engaged in a seafaring life, but he doubtless acquired his tastes at the old pier at Nairn, where a considerable trade was carried on partly by coasting vessels, partly by steamers, which passed up and down the Moray Firth, landing goods and passengers by means of boats. His translation to a shipowner's office served to quicken his desires. His new employer was an enterprising, speculative man, engaged in ventures both at home and abroad. There must have been something in the boy to command confidence, for he was again entrusted with responsible work. It must have been a curious sight to see this youth of twelve or thirteen following the ships from port to port and transacting business with all the gravity of mature years. He tells us how on one occasion he appeared as a witness in a case at Dublin. At the age of fourteen he was apprenticed on board a schooner plying on the Moray Firth. He was so anxious to be off to sea that he took the earliest opportunity that offered rather than wait for a better class of ship about which negotiations were going on. He went to sea with the sanction of his parents, though their consent was only given after it was seen that nothing but a nautical life would satisfy him. The first voyage brought him face to face with the hardships of his new mode of service, but they did not impair his resolution. He had a natural passion for the sea which never left him.

John duly served his apprenticeship, and then returned for a short time to school, to prepare himself for eventually rising to the higher ranks of his profession. He has related a curious adventure into which he was led by a daring comrade before either was out of his teens. His own ambition, however, took a wider scope. On leaving the Moray Firth trade, he served as a sailor before the mast on an Australian clipper. By-and-bye he went up for examination and passed as second mate. His first term as an officer was passed in an American ship, and his second in a British emigrant vessel. As he says himself, "In good ships sailing from one part of the world to another, I served my time as second mate, then took first mate's certificate, and finally passed as master and got a command." His master's certificate is dated in 1864.

For over twenty years after this time, Captain Bain was in command of large vessels engaged in the foreign and colonial trade. At an early stage of his career he became commodore captain of the County Line sailing from Glasgow. The trade was chiefly between Java and Holland, carried on in splendid vessels. Captain Bain was proud of his last sailing ship the "County of Nairn," which was acknowledged to be one of the smartest sailing vessels of the time. His first steamer was the "County of Sutherland," which was intended to be the pioneer of a line to be also employed in the Java trade. "Standing," he says, "on the bridge of this magnificent steamer of 3000 tons, as we proceeded down the Clyde on the trial trip, I could not help recalling my first voyage in the little smack 'Mary' and wondering what my dear mother thought of it all now." His mother, a sagacious, gentle, and well-informed woman, lived to a good old age and rejoiced in her son's success. He had been for years in command of steamers before she passed away. It is unnecessary to follow Captain Bain throughout his career as a master mariner; it is sufficient to say that he commanded in all seas, often in circumstances that tested his nerve and skill, and that he never met with a serious misfortune. His last experiences at sea were as captain of a vessel of the Clan Line. While occupying this post, he carried the 2nd Regiment of Beloochees from Kurrachi to Suez to take part in the Egyptian Expedition. On that occasion he received the thanks of the military authorities for the expeditious and efficient manner in which he accomplished the transfer of the troops. The compliment was enhanced to him by the fact that it came through a distinguished countryman of his own, General Sir Herbert Macpherson, who at the time commanded the Indian Contingent, both being connected with the town of Nairn. Captain Bain brought back the 4th Madras Native Infantry to India, and was presented by the officers with a handsome set of bronzes as an acknowledgement of his great kindness and attention to all the troops on board his vessel.

Captain Bain's acquaintance with the life and work of a seaman in all its departments made him a sympathetic and considerate commander. By nature he was as firm as he was courteous. If it was necessary to reprimand he did not hesitate to discharge his duty but his words left no bitterness. His idea of the duty of a commander was to maintain strict discipline in every department of the ship, and to be ever on his part against the tendency to laxity or overconfidence in navigation. In difficult situations he was conspicuous for readiness of resource. In the autumn of 1883, when a slight mishap occurred through the blunder of a pilot, a Ceylon planter took occasion to write a letter to the newspapers respecting the "Clan Macintosh" and its captain. "I had the good fortune," he said, "when a sailor, to serve many years under Captain Bain's command, and I would rather trust myself with him in charge of the ship than all the other captains I served under put together. Everywhere he went he was a favourite with children and grown-up people. I have weathered many a gale with him, and never once did he lose his presence of mind; even when all on board thought their last hour had come, his voice was heard clear above the gale giving his orders as cool as though nothing was wrong. This is the sort of man that sailors have full confidence in. If the Clan Line have many men like him in command of their ships, they are to be congratulated. If I had always had the good luck to have sailed under the command of gentlemen like Captain Bain, I do not think I would ever have turned planter even with (at that time) the tempting offer of a coffee estate if I would leave the sea." About the same time as this letter was written, the passengers on board the "Clan Macintosh" presented an address to Captain Bain expressing their high esteem and their desire in future to travel, if possible, under his friendly care.

In 1885 Captain Bain, having been married for some years, retired from the sea, and along with his friend Captain Stobo opened a surveyor's office in Glasgow. Soon afterwards he was appointed one of the Nautical Assessors in Board of Trade inquiries throughout the United Kingdom. He was the first Scottish sailor who had ever been appointed to the office. On the passing of the new Nautical Assessors (Scotland) Act he was appointed an assessor in maritime causes in the Court of Session, and held appointments in the Sheriff Courts of Lanark, Renfrew, and other counties. These positions he was eminently qualified to fill by his varied experience and his sound practical judgment. During his residence in Glasgow, Captain Bain took an active part in much useful public work. He was one of the leading organisers of the Lifeboat Saturday Demonstrations, and lectured on behalf of the Institution in various parts of the country. A conspicuous feature of his character was his disregard of self-interest, and his eager desire to help other people, especially young men from Nairn and its neighbourhood. When in command of a ship he was always ready to advance the interests of promising lads, and in Glasgow he put himself to no end of trouble for the same object. The case of a young man from his brother's newspaper office in Nairn, who went to the great city in search of work, may be mentioned by way of example. Writing on the occasion of Captain Bain's death, this young man said :—" Captain Bain was always my ideal of what a Nairn man away from home should be. I cannot forget his great kindness to myself. When I went to Glasgow six years ago, and had to make the round of the offices in search of work, I faced the situation with that shivering sense of smallness and incapacity which affects most countrymen when first they find themselves on the steps of a daily. Captain Bain went round with me and introduced me everywhere. I was never more grateful for anything." The Rev. Mr Martin, Nairn, supplies another instance that came to his knowledge. "A Nairn lad had enlisted Captain Bain's help to find him a place as a clerk, and while they went the round of the offices in quest of a situation, he casually remarked that he had a brother serving as an engineer whose time would be up a year later, and who would then be looking out for a place as a journeyman. You may judge of that lad's feelings when a few weeks before the year was up he received a letter from Captain Bain telling him he had been kept in mind and that a situation was ready for him." Hundreds of other young men have similar stories to tell.

During his life Captain Bain kept up a close connection with the town of Nairn. In the interval of sea voyages he spent his holidays with his brother (Mr George Bain of the "Nairnshire Telegraph") and his sister Miss Bain, at their residence, Rosebank. There too, after he had settled in Glasgow, Captain and Mrs Bain, with their two boys, passed the month of August every year. During these visits he assisted in any movement that happened to be going on for the benefit of the community, particularly any scheme to promote the welfare of seamen. On one occasion, during a heavy gale, he gallantly took out the lifeboat, with a volunteer crew, and rescued ten men from a Norwegian barque, which was wrecked on the Old Bar off the Culbin Sands. For this he received a medal from the King of Norway and Sweden, and the thanks of the National Lifeboat Institution.

On Captain Bain's last visit to Nairn, in the autumn of 1895, the illness from which he died had made itself painfully manifest. In the beginning of that year he was seized with influenza, which undermined his strong and buoyant constitution. From this attack he never fully recovered. A form of heart affection developed, and after his return from Nairn to Glasgow, the disease assumed an acute form, and terminated in his death. Captain Bain passed away on the 1st of November, 1895, before he had completed his fifty-sixth year. It was felt by all his friends and acquaintances that he had been prematurely cut off. Until he was enfeebled by influenza, his life had been one of constant activity; and even after his illness had made progress, it was difficult for him to restrain his efforts within the necessary limits. He was a man of high principle and fine feeling, and of profound though unostentatious religious faith. He was connected as a deacon with the Free High Church at Partick, and took his full share of work as an officebearer of the congregation.

The people of Nairn desired that the remains of a townsman whom they held in such respect should be honoured with a public funeral. The interment took place in the Nairn Cemetery on 6th November. The Provost, Magistrates and Town Council walked in front, and a large concourse followed the hearse. The shops and public offices were closed, and the blinds drawn on the windows along the route. The ships in the harbour hoisted their flags half-mast high. Rev. Mr Martin, minister of the Free Church, conducted the services. The pallbearers were George Bain, elder son of the deceased; George Bain, Rosebank, brother; G. B. Mackintosh, Seabank; W. Mackintosh, Inverness; G. B. Mackintosh, Rose Cottage, Nairn; James Barron,

Inverness; Colonel Fraser, Redheugh; J. D. Lamb, National Bank; and W. Lightbody, Kingillie. A number of beautiful wreaths were placed on the grave from friends, including one from Sir Robert Finlay, Solicitor-General for England, and Lady Finlay, in affectionate remembrance.

Numerous expressions of regret at the death of Captain Bain were received by his friends. Sir Robert Finlay wrote—"I have very special cause to remember him. His high character and great capacity made a strong impression upon me, and I can never forget the great kindness I received at his hands." His own clergyman, Rev. Dr Bremner, made special reference to him from the pulpit. "Every movement," he said, "for the welfare of seamen, whether temporal or spiritual, had in him a warm supporter. He took a deep interest in the widows and orphans of sailors, and his labours in the Lifeboat movement—often, I fear, beyond his strength—are still fresh in the recollection of most of us. Captain Bain in his voyages round the world had seen many lands and many peoples, and nothing delighted him more than to impart to an audience of young people somewhat of his rich store of nautical experience, or to exhibit to them by means of the lantern the scenes he had witnessed in far-off countries. Rarely have I known a more manly, more genial, and withal more Christian man and it is, I am sure, to all of us a great grief that we shall look upon his face no more." An old friend, Mr John Mackintosh, Inverness, who had known Captain Bain from boyhood, wrote—"His career was one of great brilliancy and usefulness, and he carried his high Christian principles into daily life, which is the grand idea of our lives." From many other friends, including the late Sir Thomas Brodie, and the Rev. Mr Lee, came expressions of equal esteem and cordiality. The Rev. Mr Martin, who had been but recently settled in Nairn, spoke of the impression which had been made upon himself. "As a stranger," he said, "I have been much struck with the unanimous tribute of affection paid by this community to his memory. Every man seems to feel that in him he has lost a friend. It is a striking proof of the power of a great and good character that, despite his long years of residence elsewhere, he was able to hold so large a place in the hearts of the people here."

Captain Bain was married in 1882 to Charlotte,

daughter of Captain James Marshall of the Inniskilling Dragoons, who survives him, along with two boys. In his married life he was particularly happy. The Reminiscences which form the present volume were written at intervals in his busy career. They will be read with interest by those who knew him, and, it is believed, by many others who may obtain from them some real knowledge of the nature and circumstances of a seafaring life.

The present writer has penned with peculiar pleasure this brief but inadequate tribute to the memory of one of the most lovable men he has ever known—one who added to the possession of a clear intellect and a firm will, the higher graces of a tender, affectionate, and upright nature.

JAMES BARRON.

INVERNESS, *20th February*, 1897.

CHAPTER I.

INTRODUCTORY.

From my earliest years, my great desire was to be a sailor. I cannot account for my liking for a sailor's life. None of my own people had any connection with the sea, and I had associated very little with seafaring folk. To me, however, the fairest vision on earth was the sight of the little barks passing up and down the Moray Firth; and even when ardently engaged in boyish sports on the Links of Nairn—my native town—the appearance of a ship under sail, or of a boat rowing out of the harbour, set my fancy a-working on pictures of the life of a sailor.

My first introduction to the fisher-folk of Nairn was somewhat amusing. I had when eleven years of age become junior clerk in the office of the inspector of poor, and part of my duty was to deliver the tax-papers to the ratepayers and collect the rates from those ready to pay. I got on fairly well as a tax-gatherer till I came to the fishertown. My difficulties then became overwhelming. The entire fisher population in Nairn have really but one surname—that of "Main." They are distinguishable, even amongst themselves, only by the use of "tee-names." Thirty or forty persons answer to the name of "John Main." I had tax-papers for all of them. The houses were irregularly built, and the name of the street was no sure guide. The fisher-folk had a decided aversion to paying taxes, so I got no assistance from them. On the contrary, they did all they could to perplex and bewilder me, and refused to accept my papers. On entering a narrow close I discovered one rascal busily rubbing out the numbers on the door-lintels with a white-wash brush. I returned to the office, considerably crestfallen, with a large bundle of undelivered notices. The inspector listened to my tale of woe. "Go back to-morrow morning," he said, "and if they don't take the paper out of your hand pitch it on the floor, and leave them to find out who it is intended for. Catch one of them paying a penny more than is his due!" I did as I was told, and sure enough the plan succeeded. When they saw I was not to be done this time, they speedily engaged in the work of exchanging papers and otherwise redding up the confusion of names, and all the notices ultimately found their proper destination.

Before very long the fisher-folk and I became better acquainted. One day of oppressive dulness in the office, the inspector, discerning doubtless by my wearied looks that I was becoming tired of my occupation, remarked—"You don't like this work, boy?" I promptly replied—"I would rather be a sailor!" "A sailor!" he exclaimed; and a strange, wistful, far-off look came into the old man's face as if the memory of an old dream had been suddenly awakened. I felt sure he had wanted to be a sailor himself at one time, and—what was more—regretted he had not followed his youthful fancy. My belief was confirmed when I found shortly after that his favourite intellectual pastime when office hours dragged was the construction of logarithms and the working of questions in navigation. He said nothing further, but I noticed he left his navigation books lying about in such a way as that I might, if so disposed, have a look at them during idle hours. My mind, however, was more intent on picturing the old inspector of poor as the commander of a great ship, with myself as his chief mate. I never could rid myself of the idea that the old gentleman had been born to be a sailor, but by some mischance had missed his destiny.

An opening in a shipowner's office gave me what I wanted—a closer connection with the sea. I felt in my element in my new sphere. My master was engaged in a pretty extensive trade as an importer of coals and lime, and an exporter of timber and other local produce. It was a time when the minds of a few energetic men in the North of Scotland had awakened to the possibilities of a lucrative trade by sea between North and South, and my master was the boldest and most adventurous spirit among them. Nothing steadies a youth like responsibilities. Although only a boy of twelve years of age, I was entrusted with loading and discharging the vessels, following them from port to port in the Moray Firth, and receiving and paying large sums of money. I thought nothing about it at the time, but I have often wondered since how any man could have entrusted one of my age with such important affairs, not merely with the safety of the money, but with the transaction of business which often required considerable tact and judgment. I had, however, sense enough to know that my youth was against me in matters of business, but I endeavoured to make amends by being frank, respectful, and obliging to everybody. The first thing was to know what was best for my master's interests; the second was to make friends. And so I got on famously. A slip of a boy riding about on a greyfaced pony, with his pockets filled with charter-parties, bank bills, cheques, and pound notes, I came to be a pretty familiar figure round the head of the Moray Firth during the early "Fifties," and when it was found I knew what I was about, I came to be accepted and dealt with as a responsible agent.

Once only did I find my youth to be a reproach. A smack, named "The Mary," went ashore one night on the Whiteness Head—a sandspit near Fort-George. She was laden with herrings. All the seafaring worthies of the place—and they were a funny lot, many of them—were engaged to get the vessel off the sandbank. I was there as time-keeper and general administrator. After weeks of hard work, day and night, on the lonely sandbank, we succeeded in surrounding the craft by innumerable empty beer barrels, lashed together and fastened to the hull at low water. We had also a couple of old boats tommed down under her main boom which was placed amidships. We waited for the spring-tide. It came, and along with it a gale of wind from the N.E. The barrels broke adrift and the boats were doubled up. The "Mary" remained fast in her bed of sand. We were in despair, and contemplated abandoning the vessel as a wreck. During the time I was on the scene, I had made the acquaintance of the son of a farmer in the neighbouring Carse. He was the herd-boy, but a most intelligent, ingenious lad, and he suggested to me a way of floating her. Next morning I sent for a quantity of plasterer's lath-board and tarred canvas. We nailed the boards and the canvas over the seams of the vessel, and she rose at once with the flood tide. I got great credit for the happy expedient, but it was really Donald Macpherson, herd-boy in the Carse of Delnies, who was the inventor of this appliance in ship-raising. Many years after, I narrated my first experience in ship-raising to a famous ship-raiser, and he remarked that the first method was as good as any that could have been adopted in the circumstances, but the lath and canvas was a new idea which he begged leave to make a note of. The cargo of herrings, which had been discharged on the beach, was sold by public auction for the benefit of whom it might concern. I bought the lot for £300, and the purchase was put down in my name. The vessel, properly repaired, reloaded the herrings and sailed for Ireland. Disputes arose respecting the ownership of the cargo, and litigation in the Irish Courts followed.

I was summoned to Dublin to give evidence. My purchase of the herrings, in the first instance, involved an important point in the case, and the court adjourned till my arrival. I caught the mail coach for the South, and crossed over by steamer to Dublin. It was my first glimpse of the great outer world. When I was ushered into the witness-box, I noticed some of the learned gentlemen of the Bar smiling at my appearance. I had bought a new overcoat before starting from home: it was much too long for me, and I thought they must be making fun of it. The Judge adjusted his spectacles, and looking at me, asked in the severest tones, "Who is this?" The Court roared with laughter. "Are you the—ah—gentleman we have heard so much about in this case who bought a cargo of herrings at the Whiteness Head for £300?" I promptly replied, "I am, my Lord." "What is your age?" "Thirteen years, my Lord"—a declaration which caused renewed merriment in Court. "Is it usual for boys of your age in Scotland to engage in such extensive commercial speculations?" I assured his Lordship that I had purchased timber repeatedly to a much greater value on my own responsibility. He drew from me a great many particulars of my work as shipping-clerk, and how I had frequently to buy and sell, to the best advantage, according to my own judgment. In the case of the cargo of herrings, I had been instructed to buy the herrings if they went at a reasonable price. I think his Lordship was favourably disposed towards me. Our own Counsel gave me a most flattering character, and stated (which was not quite true) that but for me the ship "Mary" and her cargo would still have been on the Whiteness Head. The Counsel for the opposite side, however, declared that it was a fortunate circumstance that I had been produced in Court, as it confirmed his contention that the sale had been an attempt at fraud, for who, he asked, would believe that a boy of thirteen years of age could be a *bona fide* purchaser of a cargo of herrings? We lost the case, on the ground that I was too young to be regarded as a responsible purchaser.

My visit to Ireland intensified my desire to become a sailor. There was one great barrier—my mother refused her consent. Strong as was my desire to go to sea, there was one attachment still stronger, and unless she had given her permission I would never have put a foot on board a ship. Running away to sea was not to my taste. I felt that I could never be happy if I left broken hearts behind me, and my observation has since been that without the feeling of home ties, a lad is deprived of one of the strongest incentives to do right. So I waited on. Perceiving at length that it was no mere fancy but a strong passion I had formed for a seafaring life, my good mother one day took me aside and told me she would no longer oppose my going to sea. It cost her a great struggle, I know. She sacrificed her dearest wishes to my inclination, and the thought of it put me on my mettle.

CHAPTER II.

ON BOARD A COLLIER.

Any one looking at a collier vessel as she lies in the harbour, her decks blackened and her rigging smutty with coal dust, and the sailors and shore-labourers heaving wearily all day long at the winch, might well think there was very little to attract in the life on board such a vessel. But wait till she clears the pier-heads, and sets her sails to the breeze. Then come in all the pleasure and exhilaration of yacht-sailing. He is a dull fellow who is not wakened up by the freshness and buoyancy of the first hour's sail from port. Then the watch is set. Duties are assigned, and the sense of responsibility arising from allotted work comes into play, and there is just the same feeling of rank and rating in the small schooner as in the biggest ship afloat. The captain, as befits him, stands aloof; the mate has his own distinct position; and the crew—well, they feel that if they are a step or two below the status of the captain and mate, they are vastly superior to the lad who does the cooking. Discipline and order prevail in the smallest craft. And so the collier goes on her passage from port to port, manned by an organised ship's company, who regard the navigation of their little vessel as the most important concern in the universe.

My first voyage as a sailor was from Nairn to Newcastle, in a coasting smack. The start was to me discouraging and disappointing. The weather was fearfully rough, and I was dreadfully sick. For a week or more I suffered from the *mal de mer*, and when my watch on deck was up there was little inducement to go below to the wretched little foc'sle, with its, to me, abominable smell of tobacco and tar. My experience during these days convinced me that I had chosen a rough road in life. Sunday morning was ushered in with a perfect tempest. The little craft was tossed about like a fleck of foam on the ocean. At daybreak we got inshore close to Berwick-on-Tweed, where the water was smooth. The scene I beheld a few hours later caused me more sinking of heart than even the tossing of the angry waves of the North Sea. There was the land, the town, the hills—a picture of perfect peace and repose. I could hear the church bells ringing, and could see the people in groups wending their way thither, and my thoughts went back to home—to the church and the Sunday school—every detail of the quiet, happy life I had left behind me came flashing back. I confess if I could have got ashore that morning I would have abandoned a seafaring life for ever. But there was no way of escape, and I presently found myself lending a hand in getting the smack to go about and face the restless, raging sea. It was the only time I ever had any regret at having chosen a sailor's life. The feeling of despondency and depression never recurred again, even in the most trying circumstances.

I served my regular apprenticeship in a Banff schooner. I had an advantage as a sailor in having had a hand in rigging out the vessel. For some months, off and on, we were engaged setting up the rigging, and one forms a peculiar attachment to a ship whose every rope, sail, and spar you have seen prepared and placed in the craft. "The Lady Abercromby"—such was her name—was one of the smartest schooners on the coast, and Captain Yell who sailed her as good a coasting skipper as one could possibly have served under. He inspired me with the true sailor's ideal to have everything on board one vessel ship-shape, never forgetting the importance of doing little things well. On my apprenticeship being up, I left the "Lady Abercromby." Not very long after, she was wrecked on the Aberdeenshire coast, and poor Captain Yell and my old shipmates were drowned.

My apprenticeship finished, I counted myself a smart sailor, able to hold my own with most in practical seamanship, but I was quite conscious that if ever I was to get on in my profession I must give some time to the study of navigation. Accordingly I returned to school in my native town. A full-fledged sailor, entitled to write the letters "A.B." after his name, was regarded by the schoolboys somewhat as a *rara avis*. They used to gather round my corner, listening to my yarns, to the decided detriment of the prosecution of their school lessons. There was no regular class to go into, but the schoolmaster arranged that I should study trigonometry and mathematics with the senior pupil who was preparing for the entrance examination for the Royal Engineers. Of navigation the worthy schoolmaster knew nothing, and I had to teach myself anything I learned of that subject. The few months spent in this way were not wasted, and when some years later I had seriously to tackle navigation as a subject of examination, I found myself quite familiar with the technical formulæ. Curiously enough, my fellow-student in trigonometry and I met at the opening of the Manchester Canal—he a Colonel in the Royal Engineers, and holding an important post at the War Office, and I, an Ancient Mariner holding an appointment from the Home Office.

My intention was to have joined a foreign-going vessel as soon as I had finished my little spell at school, but I was drawn into one of the most reckless and foolhardy enterprises imaginable. I made the acquaintance of a young fellow named James Wilson, who was mate of one of the schooners belonging to Nairn. Although we were townfellows, I had never happened to come across him before. Wilson was one of the most fascinating characters I have ever met in my career. Small in stature but very shapely in build, and of a clear bright complexion, he had a most winning manner, and, as I came to know afterwards, an indomitable spirit. His yellow wavy hair and incipient moustache made him look younger than he was, but there was nothing effeminate about him. Wilson one day informed me that he had been offered the command of a ship, and asked me if I would go with him as mate. He explained that while he would be master, the mate and man who joined him would share equally with him in the venture. In short, his proposal was that three of us should man the schooner "Speedwell," and divide the profits with the owner. I suggested that we would probably be laid hold of by the law and committed as lunatics, as the ship to be properly manned would require five hands at least. Wilson would accept no refusal:—were we not equal singly to any two ordinary seamen? he would ask. The end of it was that he became the captain, I the mate, and Daniel Main the crew of the good ship "Speedwell." And a rare time we had of it. There was certainly a spice of romance and adventure in the affair. How we knocked about the old craft was wonderful. Our madcap proceedings, as many were pleased to regard our way of sailing the "Speedwell," became the talk of all the seafaring folk of the Moray Firth. They re-christened the vessel "The Three Boys!" It pretty well hit the mark, for we were not out of our teens, any of us. Amused crowds used to meet us on our arrival, especially at the smaller ports, but they stopped their jeering when they discovered that "the three boys" were uncommonly good fighters as well as plucky sailors. We made a point of dressing smartly when we went ashore of an evening, so as to show no traces of the hard work we had to perform. The coasting sailor's life is full of temptations to drink, at least it was so at that time. Except at his own home, he has no friends at the ports he visits. He cannot remain all the time by his ship; and the public-house is the only open door for him. I daresay if some moralist saw the "captain, mate, and crew" of the "Speedwell" going into the "Ship Inn," as they sometimes did, he would conclude that they were young men on the highway to ruin. But the fact was we did not drink. What happened generally was this. We entered the public room and found several old skippers at their grog and pipes. Waiting only to exchange views about the weather, and declining proffered hospitality, we passed into the landlady's private parlour, and there we spent the evening in social enjoyments. Remember, reader, we were three jolly young tars to whom music and dancing had irresistible charms. Our shipmate, "Dan," I recollect, did not quite emulate his officers in their devotion to such amusements, and when the social party was fairly underweigh he used to slip out, to see, he said, that all was right with the craft. It was at such times, I believe, that he told the wonderful stories of the doings of "The Three Boys" which gained us so much notoriety. I must say a good word for those landladies. I never knew one of them who encouraged young fellows to drink. On the contrary, I have known them do all they could to restrain excess—in fact, were really very kind, good friends to the young sailor. To make up for their hospitality to us, though that was not wanted on their part, we usually gave a grand return supper to wind up with before sailing.

I have seen us many a time the light-hearted leaders of the dance at eleven at night, and before midnight out in the stormy North Sea battling for dear life. "The Three Boys" made a point of sailing whatever kind of weather was outside. Though a good sea-boat, our ship was not a particularly fast sailer, and we had to make up for it by "carrying on." The old skippers after their grog went comfortably to bed in port, in the hope of a change of weather in the morning. We slipped out with the tide, and had a try for it. We had rare luck sometimes. I remember once our giving the collier fleet who were storm-stayed in the Firth of Forth the slip in this way. It was blowing a gale outside, but we took advantage of a lull and went out to sea. We had a splendid run all the way to Inverness, where we discharged our cargo, loaded, sailed for Sunderland, discharged and loaded again, and came up on the wind-bound vessels just as they were emerging out of the shelter of their haven of rest, where they had been for a full fortnight.

On one occasion we lost the ship. It was a beautiful evening, and we lay becalmed about a mile off the shore, somewhere near the Firth of Forth. Wilson had exhausted his feats of diving and swimming. He was the boldest swimmer I have ever met. His dog one day was swept off the deck by a heavy sea. Instantly he jumped overboard after it. Before we could round-to, the vessel had to make a circuit of a mile or two. We could just see him, a dark object on the crest of a wave. When we came up to rescue him, there was he patting his dog on the head, much more concerned for his dog's safety than for his own. But on this particular summer evening, the water was so smooth that, as he said, there was no fun to be got out of it. "What do you say to our going ashore and getting a fresh supply of milk from that farm up there?" he asked. "All right," I replied and we out boat and away ashore, leaving "Dan" in full charge. We reached the farm-house, got into the good graces of the farmer's wife, and accepted an invitation to tea with the goodwoman and her two pretty daughters. It was a delightful break in the monotony of our existence, and we parted from our fair entertainers at sun-down, promising to return next day if the wind did not waft us away. When we got to the brow of the hill we looked about for the craft, but she was nowhere to be seen. She was gone from her anchorage. We hurried down to the boat, and pulled off in the faint hope that a ship's hull just discernible on the horizon might be the "Speedwell." It was the longest pull I ever had at the oar. By dawn of next morning, we came up to the vessel—it was our own lost ship. A breeze had sprung up, and filled her sails shortly after we had gone ashore. She tripped her anchor, and to the despair of "Dan" went scudding off before the breeze. He, poor fellow, made fast the helm, paid out all the chain, and took in some sail, but all in vain. Fortunately for us the wind had died away again, enabling us to come up to her, and we thus got out of a very awkward scrape. I am sorry we never had an opportunity of explaining to our friends on the hill why we did not pay them another visit, though we more than once passed under the shadow of the cliff.

The most serious mishap which occurred to us was entirely due to Wilson's perversity in disregarding a Moray Firth tradition. He refused to "salute the Laird of Troup." One day as we were making Troup Head, the highest land on the Banffshire coast, I was telling him the story of a Yankee skipper who was told by his Banff mate that it was the recognised custom in the Moray Firth to salute the Laird of Troup in passing his house, and that any omission of this civility was resented and punished by the Laird. The Yankee captain replied —"I guess as a freeborn American I ain't goin' to salute any laird or lord in this tarnation country!" "All right," said the mate. The ship came up to Troup Head with a light breeze, and had just passed the bold headland by a quarter of a mile, when off came a squall which carried away both the Yankee's topmasts! "I told you the Laird would be displeased!" said the mate. "Well, now," said Wilson, "I am of the same mind as the Yankee skipper, and will decline this afternoon to salute the Laird of Troup." "All right," said I. Wilson took the helm himself, so that the steering would not be at fault. We had a fine fair wind and all sail set. We came abreast of Troup Head, and sure enough off came a sudden squall, which struck down our foretopmast and split two of our sails! "I told you the Laird would be displeased!" was all I said. The consequence was that we had to go into Aberdeen for repairs. All the time I was on the coast I never once omitted "saluting the Laird of Troup." Wilson also thought better of it and never objected.

How long we might have continued our reckless performance with this undermanned ship, I don't know. We were no doubt making better than ordinary wages, but I think it was the element of adventure in it which kept us at it. It turned out, however, that the owner of the craft in Newcastle had got into financial difficulties, and when we arrived there one morning we were informed that the ship was under arrest for debt, and was to be handed over to a Dutchman. So we had to leave and find our way north, with just as much money and no more as paid our passages. Wilson and I were together in another ship, "Lord Hill," but finally we parted, never to meet again. He eventually became captain of a barque on the coast of Australia, and paid the penalty of his reckless daring by keeping his ship at sea until she foundered, though a harbour of refuge lay close at hand to which he could have run. I also left the coast, but not before I had one experience I was not likely soon to forget.

I became mate of the schooner "Albion," and on a voyage from the Moray Firth to Newcastle we were caught in a tremendous gale after rounding Peterhead. For three weeks we were battered about in the North

Sea. Gale succeeded gale, and we lost our reckoning. Our spars were carried away, and nearly all the sails split into ribbons. To make matters worse, our provisions ran done. In the midst of a terrific gale on a good Sunday morning we saw a bright light to leeward. We took it to be a shore light. We were driving helplessly towards it, and felt there was no escape for us. We had struggled in vain. In an hour hence, we would be dashed against the rocks. We fancied we heard the surge of the sea booming against the iron-bound coast. It was a dreadful thing one's end being so near, but somehow perfect peace filled one's heart. We calmly prepared for the end. After flattening out the try sail, we went below, a company of five doomed sailors. I dressed myself in my Sunday clothes. I wrote a few words saying who I was, and fastened the paper inside my coat, wondering all the while when and where and by whom I would be picked up. I also put a few lines in a bottle, stating our condition, sealed it up, and committed it to the mercy of the waves. We spent the next half-hour silently reading our Bibles. Every man dropped on his knees to his devotions. These over, we went up on deck ready for the fatal stroke. We had arranged to bid each other good-bye at the last moment. One poor fellow, the youngest of the crew, placed his hand affectionately on my shoulder as I had my foot on the companion ladder, and said with intense feeling—
"I am awfully sorry for you, Jack, with your home ties. I have none, and it does not matter for me. My father

and grandfather were lost at sea, and it seems natural I should too, but I am awfully sorry for you!" He was a rough lad, but he had a brave heart, thinking of another and not of himself at that moment. A minute later, this youth was frantic with joy, shouting—"The light has moved! the light has moved! Look, look, the bearance has shifted! It can't be a shore light! Hurrah, we are not going to be lost!" And sure enough the light had travelled. It was not a shore light. We were in God's mercy reprieved. It was probably the light of a steamer stopped on account of the head sea. The sea continued very heavy, but when daylight came the dreaded land was not to be seen. We rode out the storm, and a few days later when the ragged, tattered, battered little craft was towed up the Tyne, with her crew of starving sailors brought back from the verge of despair, we got a hearty cheer from the shore people. We learned that scores of far finer vessels had gone down in the disastrous gale, and that we had been given up for lost two weeks before the eventful Sunday morning. At home, prayers had been offered up in the churches for the safety of the "Albion" and her crew. The news of our safe arrival reached home, strangely enough, in the postscript of a letter of condolence. The coal merchant was in the act of closing a letter of sympathy to the sorrowing friends at Nairn, when a clerk rushed in with the news that we were coming up the river. There was no time to write a fresh lettter, but he added a P.S.—" Thanks be to the Almighty, our friends have this moment arrived in safety!" One can imagine the joy that postscript gave. The bottle to which I had committed the tale of our apparently impending doom turned up on the coast of Norway some months after, and I had the peculiar pleasure of reading my own message from the sea.

Experiences such as I have described are not uncommon on the coast. The little schooners encounter many a fierce gale, and the crews which man them display endurance and courage of no ordinary degree. I never regretted that my experience began on the coast. There is no better school for a sailor than the stormy North Sea. The best sailors I have ever known were bred on the East Coast of Scotland. To learn to beat up the Moray Firth is a good lesson in ship-sailing. The great drawback in beginning in a coaster for a youth who has an ambition to rise in the seafaring profession is the shortness of the voyages, which, along with the undoubted hardships he endures, makes him disinclined to put forth any serious effort to qualify himself for a higher service. There is the further disadvantage that a young fellow brought up on the coast must almost of necessity go before the mast when he joins a big ship—not the best of schools as things go nowadays. Still there is nothing to prevent any coaster lad, who has the pluck and the capacity, to attain to the position of commander of the biggest steamer afloat. He is generally a good sailor to begin with;—the rest depends upon himself; at least I found it so.

CHAPTER III.

BEFORE THE MAST.

My first start in a big ship was fairly propitious. Coming out of a small craft, whose masts would hardly make yards for the full-rigged Australian clipper I had now joined, I felt for the first twenty-four hours as if I had never been on board a ship before, everything appeared to me to be on so gigantic a scale. This feeling, however, soon wore off, and by keeping my eyes open I soon got familiar with my new surroundings. So well did I affect the *role* of an old hand that I passed the scrutiny of the "forecastle," who never suspected that I was a "greenhorn." It was well for me, as otherwise I would have been subjected to some disagreeable experiences.

The focs'le of a big ship in its own way is sometimes as companionable and enjoyable a place as any other department of the vessel—at other times it is the reverse. Thirty-six of us were crowded into a very narrow space. We were a mixed lot, and might be roughly divided into three classes—good fellows, queer chaps, and bad characters. I think nearly all of us were strangers to each other, but sailors don't need formal introductions. The division into watches was the first line drawn. I was picked for the mate's watch. The first stormy night practically settled the status of each man in the focs'le. Up till that time, the cheekiest fellows took pre-eminence and laid down the law, but the order of superiority was finally settled on the yard-arms in a squall of wind when all hands were called out to reef sail. It was then I first knew the pull I had over most of the big-ship sailors by my experience in the North Sea. Close beside me on the yard was a fellow about my own age from Shetland. He too knew what he was about, having had a similar training, and instead of the mate shouting to us, "Why don't you do —" this, that, and the other thing, he paid us the compliment of saying, "Well done, lads!"—I suppose we merited it, for the mate was more given to cursing than blessing. When we next mustered on the focs'le-head every man's qualities as a sailor were known and recognised. The tall talkers almost to a man were nowhere. Another thing happened a week or two afterwards. The captain called the Shetland lad and myself aft one day, and said—"Look here! I hate bad steering, and there has been too much of it on board this ship. Now I am going to make you quarter-masters from this time out, and see that you make a good course." He did the same in the second mate's watch, picking out two fine young fellows; and, such is human nature, the four quarter-masters from that moment regarded themselves as the aristocracy of the focs'l—we did not get a separate "house"—and formed a distinct caste by ourselves. It turned out that four of us had gone to sea from fancy rather than from any necessity or compulsion.

Away from drink and under proper discipline, the motley crew improved greatly, and with the exception of three or four incorrigible rascals, the ship's company forward was not at all bad. This being my first foreign voyage, I used to enjoy drawing out the old sailors into telling yarns. On a fine night, when the vessel had been snugged down and was bowling along, we always gathered in a group round the long-boat. It is at such times Jack indulges most freely his innate love of romance and song. The origin of the word "yarn" has been traced back to the time when sailors spent long weary hours spinning tow in the deck-house in wet weather, and to while away the time told each other tales of the sea. The art thus acquired has not been lost, and to have been shipmates with a man on a long voyage is to qualify you to write his biography. There are long yarns and short yarns. I have known a yarn to last a whole month, though proceeding at the rate of two or three hours per day. The story which the sailor intends relating usually forms but a small part of the yarn he spins. A short yarn usually relates to something which occurred in the last voyage; the long ones to some years ago. Stories of shipwreck or disasters at sea were the most common yarns, and three sailors in our ship's company, it appeared, had been cast on a desert island, with experiences akin to those of Robinson Crusoe. Two of my shipmates, I found, had been millionaires, and one the owner of real estate of priceless value in the City of Melbourne. Their favourite yarns related to the early rush to the Gold Diggings. In every case poor Jack had been cheated by some rascal of a shoreman.

In my watch there was a peculiar-looking old sailor who was exceedingly reticent regarding his history. His name was Seth Snow. He rarely exchanged words with any of his shipmates, and kept himself very much to himself. The belief in the focs'le was that Seth had come down in the world, and he was sometimes addressed as "Cap'n Snow!" to his evident annoyance. One night an extra hand was required at the wheel, and Seth was posted to the duty along with me. I could not help feeling sorry for the lonely old chap, but though our companionship at the wheel was agreeable enough, our intercourse ceased the moment we went off duty. Next night we were together again, and when relieved, Seth, to my surprise, proposed that we should spend our turn below on deck, as the night was going to be fine. I perceived he had something on his mind, and encouraged him to talk. He at length asked me with great eagerness if I knew the Clyde. I said I did. "And you know the Black Buoy at the Tail o' the Bank?" "Yes," I replied, "every sailor knows it." "Well," he asked, "have you ever heard any story about it? No. Well, I will tell you about it. A good many years ago the captain of a barque in the port of Quebec found himself ready for sea, but his sailors had deserted his ship. His mate, cook, and boy had gone away with the rest of the crew, leaving not a soul on board but himself. They said the captain was a tyrant and swore so dreadfully that they would not sail with such a man. It was quite true—the captain did swear a bit, but only when things were not done to his mind. But what was he to do now? The winter was drawing on, and the St. Lawrence might be frozen over any day. All the other ships had sailed—he alone was left. To be detained in Quebec over winter and his ship due at Glasgow before Christmas—his reputation as a shipmaster would be ruined. Day by day and night by night he scoured the now half-empty streets and lanes of Quebec trying to persuade seafaring men to join his ship, but in vain. Double wages would not tempt them. Going down to the wharf one night long after dark from a fruitless search for a crew, he declared to himself, with an oath, that he would sell his soul to the devil if he could only get his ship away. No sooner had he uttered the rash words than a Man in Black—tall black hat, long black coat, big black gloves—everything black—accosted him, and asked if he meant what he had just said. He spoke civilly enough, but with a slight sneer that implied a challenge of courage. The captain, being in a desperate mood, repeated the words. 'Very well, captain,' said the stranger, 'let it be a bargain betwixt us. You will give the orders for the proper navigation of the ship to me, and I will see they are carried out.' An uneasy feeling that he had gone too far arose in the captain's heart, and he bethought him of making one condition to safeguard his position. 'Will you promise to obey my orders implicitly?' 'I will!' promptly replied the Man in Black. Then they shook hands—it was a vow. They soon reached the vessel, and in a few seconds the rustling of ropes and the grating of chains indicated that she was being unmoored. Not a living creature could the captain see. He gave the orders and an invisible crew carried them out. Sails were set, the course was steered, and the ship proceeded down the St. Lawrence. Reaching the open sea, the yards were trimmed to the breeze, and the vessel sped across the Atlantic. So perfectly was everything done, that for the first time in his life the old captain had no call to grumble, far less to swear, as he used to do at his sailors. As the voyage began to near its termination, the captain began to reflect on the awful bargain he had in a moment of despair made. With the Man in Black, he had held no conversation, beyond telling him what to do in navigating the ship. As to the identity of the personage with whom he was associated he had no manner of doubt, for had he not seen him at the cabin table, night after night, playing cards with an invisible partner? Land on the starboard bow! He must make up his mind, now or never, how he was to escape the clutches of his adversary. A happy thought struck him, and he decided to put it into execution. 'Get the anchors over the bows!"

he shouted, 'and see that you grease the rope cable well from end to end!' 'Aye, aye, sir,' was the reply, and the work was done in a jiffy. 'Stand by to let go the anchor, and let it run till I tell you to hold on!' 'Aye, aye, sir.' The captain began to recover his spirits. He kept every stitch of canvas on the vessel, which was going her full speed, until he was in a position to anchor. 'Put the helm hard-a-port!' 'Aye, aye, sir!' 'Now then,' shouted the captain, as he had never shouted before—'Let go the anchor!' The anchor was let go. The greased cable ran out at lightning speed, and when within a few fathoms of the end, the captain shouted to his companion—'Hold on!' The Man in Black did hold on. His body passed three times round the windlass, went through the hawse pipe into the water after the anchor, and he was seen no more. The Black Buoy at the Tail o' the Bank marks the very spot!"

"You have never heard that story before, have you?" asked my shipmate Seth Snow. "No," I said, "I never have." "Well," he said, "I, Seth Snow, was the captain of that belated Quebec barque, and nothing on earth will ever make me take command of a ship or swear at a sailor! It's my only chance!" He slipped away as soon as he had finished his weird tale, and except on one other occasion, he never told me any more yarns. We had a stowaway lad on board. He was named Jimmy Ducks. The lad was a good deal teased by the sailors, but Seth Snow and he were great friends. I was curious to know the bond of affection between them, and made bold to question Seth on the subject. He told me that he began his seafaring life as a stowaway himself, having run away from school at Boston, United States of America, and having been roughly treated, he wished to befriend as far as he could a lad in a similar plight. "Jimmy Ducks" was a born merchant. He had not been on board a week when he commenced a system of sale and barter, and when we arrived at Melbourne he was the first to clear out, with sufficient goods of a miscellaneous character to set up on shore as a ship-chandler. I think his friend Seth Snow helped him a good deal.

Amongst the queer characters on board was a darkey cook, Sambo. His yarns when he was permitted to join the group always took the form of a "testimony" of his own conversion. Sambo was a Methodist, but as he seemed too anxious to gain a reputation for sanctity, he was set down as a hypocrite. His favourite exercise was to shut himself in the galley after nightfall, and to perform his devotions sufficiently loud to be heard by the passers-by. Anytime one passed one could hear him saying that "when it pleased de Angel ob de Lord to come for Sambo, Sambo ready!" One night, a sailor, always up to mischief, proposed for a lark that Sambo's sincerity should be put to the test. He accordingly went to the galley-door, and found Sambo at his devotions, shut in, with only the light of a tallow candle to illuminate his dusky chamber. The sailor knocked loudly at the door. "Who is dere?" cried Sambo. "The

Angel of the Lord come for Sambo!" In a twinkling out went the light, and there was a noise of hurry-scurry amongst the pots and pans. Then in a trembling voice came the answer—"Please de Lord, Sambo not here! Poor Sambo died three days ago!" The darkey cook had a bad time of it for the rest of the voyage, and under the merciless chaff to which he was subjected he became a humbler man, if not a better Christian.

The singing of songs goes along with the spinning of yarns on board ship. Gathered round the focs'le-head, one shipmate after another expresses his emotions in song. We had several first-rate singers amongst us, and we could give a rattling good chorus at all times. One hears very little singing on board a small vessel, but in a big ship the sailors do most of their work to the melody of some song. Any form of words that may suggest itself at the moment will be caught up and turned into song. When the main tack requires an extra brace down, the officer of the watch will shout, "Now then, boys, strike a light!" The order will be responded to with—"Haul the bowline, so early in the morning, haul the bowline, the bowline, *haul!*" Or it may be, "Knock the man down, Johnnie, knock the man down!" A favourite long-pull song we had in setting up topsails was "Hanging Johnnie," the chorus being, "Hang, boys, *hang!*" In the matter of capstan songs we always gave a sort of full-dress rehearsal when weighing the anchor or heaving into dock, and the favourites were—"Round the Horn," "Santa Anna," and "Was you ever in the Rio Grande?" having as a chorus a few lines winding up with—"I am bound to the Rio Grande!" The words for the most part are nonsensical, but the full chorus of male voices has a fine effect when heard amidst the actual surroundings of ship life. A good singing crew is generally a good working crew. The song enables the men to pull together, and besides cheers and enlivens them at their work.

There is no reason in the world why the forecastle of a big ship should not be an attractive place for young fellows. The sailor's old grievances about "bad food and not enough of it" have been remedied. These things are now all regulated by Act of Parliament. Something remains to be done to give more light and space in the forecastle, and a good shelter in rough weather on deck. The rules of the Board of Trade as to tonnage measurement have, however, the effect of positively discouraging any such improvement by the shipowner—the more's the pity for all concerned. The majority of our ships are now splendidly found in every respect, except in the matter of accommodation for the crew.

CHAPTER IV.

AS MATE.

HAVING served long enough, as I thought, before the mast, I made up my mind to go before the Board of Trade examiner, and endeavour to pass as second mate. A few weeks at a Navigation School in Glasgow gave me the final drill in the subject of navigation which I needed. I had no doubt of being able to pass in practical seamanship. The room of the Board of Trade examiner has more terrors for poor Jack than the centre of a cyclone. A dozen of us went up, all in a state of extreme trepidation. For the first hour or so, the mental tension was extreme, and by the end of the day one felt as if reduced to a state of imbecility. The same questions if tackled on board ship would have cost us very little mental effort, but under the excitement of the occasion, the strain was enormous. I mention this as a possible explanation of the large number of failures of seamen going up for the first time—they are not used to it. However, I had the satisfaction of being one of four who passed. I felt very proud of it. The gaining of my first certificate gave me, I think, more gratification than any other distinction I may afterwards have earned.

My next business was to find a ship. I considered myself fortunate in getting an appointment in a first-class line, and went to work with right good will on board the ship at Glasgow. When Saturday afternoon came, I asked leave of the superintendent of line to go to Greenock to fetch up my clothes, and he granted my request, telling me to be sure to be at work on Monday morning. The weather for several days had been bitterly cold, and on Saturday night I was fairly knocked up. On Monday morning I was no better, and was just able to sit up in bed and write a note to the superintendent explaining my non-appearance. For the whole week I was confined to my room, but as soon as I was able I set off to Glasgow. The ship was still there, I found, and I met the superintendent. He told me very gruffly to clear out—he would listen to no explanation—any man who disappointed him once never got a chance of doing it a second time. So I lost my first appointment. I felt that rough measure had been meted out to me, but I knew that the superintendent was acting under a total misapprehension of the circumstances. It taught me, however, the lesson never to condemn a man without some evidence of delinquency, even though appearances were against him. Long years after, the same gentleman and I were brought frequently in contact, and he used to defer to my opinion in many important matters. I thought often of asking him if he remembered dismissing me from his service on that bleak December day. I knew he did not, so I abstained from giving the old gentleman any pain by recalling an unpleasant episode.

At the time, it was to me a very bitter experience. I knew the advantage of starting as an officer in a good line of ships; and it was with something of the feeling of recklessness that I accepted the appointment of second mate on board an American barque. I joined her, and we sailed from Glasgow, but brought up at the Tail o' the Bank, with the crew in rebellion, the captain and mate pacing the quarter-deck with loaded revolvers, and the police-signal flying from the masthead. The police boat came off, and fifteen of the sailors who had mutinied were sent ashore in irons. They were afterwards tried and sent to prison for six months for refusing to proceed to sea. The scene arose entirely from the want of a little tact and forbearance on the part of those in command of the vessel. The sailors, as is too often the case, had come on board the worse of liquor. The Yankee mate would make no allowance for their condition. "We never speak to a sailor twice on board an American ship—we knock him down if he doesn't obey the first order!" And certainly he was an adept at that business. The British tar, drunk though he was, would not stand that sort of treatment, and hence the row, which ended in their removal from the ship to prison. We got a second crew on board, but they were very little better than the first lot, and having got wind of what had happened to the first crew, they seemed bent on mischief. The mate did not relax in the least the severity of his treatment. When things had arrived at a critical point, I went up to the mate and told him that if he did not desist, I would go ashore and report him. He raised his revolver to fire at me, but as I looked him straight in the face without flinching he lowered his arm. With one spring I caught him, knocked his weapon out of his hand, and kicked it into the lee scupper. Some of the sailors saw what I had done, and they rushed to back me up. I had been but a very short time aft, but I knew sufficient of the discipline of a ship that the last thing an officer ought ever to do is to join the side of insubordination. The authority of the officers, right or wrong, must be maintained, otherwise all discipline is at an end. "Look here," I said to the mate, "don't let us make fools of ourselves before these men. Come into the cabin and let us settle it there." I knew I was now completely in his power if he liked to exercise it, and I was quite conscious that in interfering as I had my conduct had been of the gravest character. I spoke to him quietly and firmly, and told him that if he did not desist from his rough treatment of these men, it would end in mutiny and murder. He was no coward this Yankee mate. He surveyed me with a cool, contemptuous look, and would at that moment have liked nothing better than to have had a fair-and-square fight with me. "Give me these men for half-an-hour to get underweigh," I said, "and then you may do as you like." "All right" he replied, "we will settle our little accounts afterwards." I jumped out, and shouted out, "Heave up the anchor!" "Aye, aye, sir," was the ready response. Each man flew to his work with a will. I fancy they supposed that I had done for both the skipper and mate and was now in full command. The ship was underweigh in a trice, and we went sailing away as if we were the smartest ship that ever left the Clyde. The angry passions subsided, and within twenty-four hours the whole ship's company, both fore and aft, was on the most cordial terms. I found my chief officer to be a splendid fellow, highly educated, well-mannered, and kind-hearted to a degree—in short, one of the best of men I have ever sailed with, but he had an extraordinary contempt for a common sailor. In talking over the matter with him, I learned that the kind of discipline he was enforcing on the vessel prevailed universally in American ships. "We have to establish a rule of terror over the sailor before we can command obedience," he said. "What right have these sailors to come on board drunk, imperilling the lives and property entrusted to my care? They have a duty to perform, and it is my business to see that they do it." I admitted he was perfectly right in principle, but a man must be guided by circumstances as to how he is to enforce discipline among a lot of men who have rendered themselves incapable of work by drink. The mate was himself a strict abstainer, and I found that a large majority of the American skippers and officers I afterwards came to know in all parts of the world were, like him, teetotallers. As to the crew, they were on the whole an excellent set of men when sober, and the voyage which began so inauspiciously turned out very pleasantly for all.

I have said nothing of the captain thus far. He was a type of man exceedingly rare at sea—a perfect aristocrat. Had he been the Admiral in command of the American Navy he could not have been more dignified and impressive in his demeanour. It was entirely beneath his notice to take any cognisance of the ship's affairs. At stated times, the chief officer made reports to him of the distance run and the course steered, but beyond that he took no concern with the navigation of the ship. He left all these matters to his chief officer. He dressed regularly for dinner, and, in short, conducted himself as if he was a man of regal rank who happened to be a passenger on board. Though probably not carrying it to the pitch which the captain of this barque did, I gathered that this style of thing is greatly affected by the captains in American ships. The chief officer is really the sailing-master, and the captain is there merely to be consulted should any difficulties arise. He was certainly the grandest swell I ever sailed under. I believe the explanation of all this style is that the American captain is generally the principal owner of the ship, or it belongs to his family.

One of the most singular incidents in my experience happened on this voyage across the Atlantic. We were sailing to the westward with the wind SW., and were nearing the Banks of Newfoundland, when suddenly the wind came away furiously from the NW. So sudden was the blast, the sails were frozen stiff to the yards from truck to deck and could not be taken in. It was very odd to see the sailors beating the sails with handspikes and pouring hot water into the blocks and fair leads for the braces. Fortunately the gale lasted only a few hours. By daybreak, however, we were surrounded on all sides as far as the eye could reach by huge blocks of field ice, and we remained in this icy prison for over ten days. Some sixteen of the crew were frost-bitten while engaged cutting the ice into blocks on the deck and launching them overboard, and several of them had to have their fingers amputated on arrival at Halifax, Nova Scotia. A frozen ship at sea has a strange ghostly appearance. Instead of being a thing of life, she looks like a stiffened corpse. Her elasticity is gone. Every spar, rope, chain, and line is encased by a covering of rigid ice. Huge icicles hang pendant from the yards, the bowsprit bends with the heavy mass of ice adhering to it and ever accumulating as she dips. When the fresh comes, the water pours overhead in a thousand rills, like a shower bath. It is grand to see every hour giving fresh life and 'vigour to the paralysed and stiffened limbs, until she bounds once more, free and unfettered, on her onward course.

As soon as I got the chance, I exchanged the "Stars and Stripes" of the United States for the British flag, and found myself second mate of an emigrant ship bound for New South Wales. From an officer's point of view, an emigrant vessel is, on the whole, the best he can sail with. Any extra work is more than compensated for by the social intercourse he enjoys with the passengers. It has a civilising effect on a man who has spent most of his years away from the society of friends. In the course of a long voyage, life on board a passenger ship becomes very much a representation of life in a small town, with all the social incidents magnified in interest.

A week's good running with a smart ship takes us beyond the range of the stormy Atlantic gales. Having passed Madeira, we get the NE. trade winds. All sail is set. Indeed we set sails here which are never seen on ships near the land. The vessel becomes a little cloud of canvas. A sail is set in every opening to catch every breath of air. Hundreds of yards of canvas are laced on to the ordinary standing sails. Booms are rigged out on both sides on almost every yard. Under this press of canvas we go gaily along, never shifting sheet or tack for days and weeks on end. There is no change in the weather, nor in the sky, nor in the colour of the water. Land, of course, we see none. One day is as like another as possible.

This part of the voyage is always pleasant, and passengers enjoy themselves immensely, getting up all sorts of games and amusements, such as judge and jury trials, debating societies, amateur newspapers, concerts, dances, theatricals and the like. These winds carry us within a few hundred yards of the Equator, and end in a dead calm. The scene certainly changes. All the fair-wind sails are now taken down. Our object now is to have the yards clear for swinging in order to catch every puff of wind which may blow from either side. But with it all we make little or no progress. On this voyage, we lie becalmed for fourteen days. The sea is like a sheet of glass, and the sun pours out its scorching rays. The sky may be clear or dark, but there is not a breath of wind stirring. The surface of the water teems with animalculæ, but no sound breaks the stillness in sea or sky. Our feathered friends have deserted us, and even the flutter of the flying-fish is awanting. Nature seems profoundly asleep. The sound of one's voice is like an echo from a ghostly vault. A creak from a rusty yard-sling is a welcome relief from the terrible monotony. We are alone, yet we are in company, for here and there at the distance of a mile or two, sometimes nearer, sometimes further off, are vessels similarily becalmed in the Doldrums. It is too tempting not to make a call on our neighbours, and as second officer the duty falls to me to take charge of one of the boats. Visits are paid and civilities exchanged. A queer scene of shopping on the principle of barter goes on. We give a bag of potatoes and a bundle of newspapers in exchange for a monkey, a parrot, or a cage of turtle-doves. It is astonishing the number of acquaintances one makes on the high seas. We meet unexpectedly, and take our departure hurriedly. For one evening dark heavy clouds bank up in huge masses—a welcome sign. The lightning darts in every conceivable form, and the thunder rolls in dreadful majesty. An impenetrable wall of cloud, black as ink, has formed from sea to sky. A loud noise, like the howling of the wind in a forest, is heard. But, strangely enough, not a breath of wind reaches us. By and bye two huge horns are thrown out as feelers from this mountain of cloud. In a moment the ship is heeling to the breeze. The idle sails are now strained to their utmost. The whole mass of cloud passes over us, so close and heavy that you feel as if the very heavens had descended and were enveloping you in a shroud of vapour. It lasts only an hour or two, but we chance to get a fair wind from another quarter—a breeze which carries us across the Equator. The old practices connected with crossing the line were duly observed. The sailors get an hour or two of good fun, and the passengers appear to enjoy it.

Two babies were born in the steerage shortly after we had crossed the Equator. They became a never-ending source of interest and delight. The little creatures had a good deal to endure in the circumstances into which they were ushered, but the discomforts were mitigated to some extent by the kindly interest manifested in their welfare by every one on board. The cabin passengers contended with the sailors of the focs'le for possession of the babies. An understanding was ultimately arrived at by the one baby being kept aft and the other forward, week about. It is very amusing to see Jack acting as dry nurse to the baby, as he sits on the forecastle head, and meditates as to what ought to be the name of the ship's baby. One suggests the name of the ship, another the nearest headland. It ended by the girl being christened Victoria, and the boy Sydney! A baby born at sea is supposed by the sailors to have a charmed life against all the dangers of the deep.

Love-making on board ship goes on very merrily, and engagements become quite the rule. In one instance, it led to a marriage. We had a gentleman on board of the name of John Knox (doubtless a descendant of the great Reformer) who fell deeply in love with a lady passenger who was going out to be married to a Colonial gentleman and was in charge of his brother. John Knox was anxious to be married right off, and the lady was nothing loth, and accordingly, to the great consternation of the would-be brother-in-law, the couple appeared before the captain one morning, and were married by him in orthodox fashion. This function the "old man" had frequently performed before, but this was probably the last time, as the power to celebrate marriages at sea was withdrawn from masters of vessels shortly after. When we arrived at our destination, the expectant bridegroom came off to the ship to meet his intended, only to find that she had left by boat five minutes before as the wife of our gallant friend John Knox.

While such happy events occur to enliven life on board ship, we are called on to perform the saddest of all duties. The news that a shipmate is dead fills every heart with sorrow and gloom. A funeral at sea is one of the most solemn of scenes. The last offices are performed at dead of night. The body is carried to the gangway, and a broad plank is placed on the rail. The ship is hove to, and the crew mustered, and in the darkness of night, with the sea surging and boiling as if anxious for its victim, the wind wailing through the rigging, and the ship pitching and straining, impatient to be released from the check of the mainyard aback, the funeral service is begun and read by the light of a few flickering oil lamps. At the close, the plank is raised, and the body slides gently into the deep. No stone marks the sailor's grave, but we live in the blessed hope of a resurrection, when the sea shall give up its dead.

The mainyard is filled and we speed along on our voyage. Happy as a ship's company is on a long voyage, the knowledge that we are approaching land awakens the imagination and stirs the emotions of passenger and sailor alike. Our good ship has carried us through gales and storms. The wind is light but fair. The lookout shouts "Land O!" Ahead and stretching along the leeside is a dark blue line visible above the horizon. As we near it, the little hilltops show their heads over the level country, proudly proclaiming land. It is midsummer weather, though by the calendar it is the month of December. The trees and grass are beautifully green, affording a pleasing prospect to the eye weary with scanning only sea and sky. Many a prayer is breathed on such occasions, acknowledging God's goodness to us poor mortals. We are steering straight for the land, which is becoming sharper in outline every minute. Our interest is excited by the jagged appearance of the coast on the one side and the smooth contour of the cliffs on the other. We hear the sea breaking on the shore—a welcome sound. An entrance now opens up, and we sail boldly in betwixt two almost perpendicular headlands, having deep water close in at their base. In a moment, a splendid scene bursts on our view. Right ahead only a few miles distant is a magnificent city, basking in a flood of sunshine. It stretches as far as the eye can reach landwards, and slopes gently towards the shore, with a fringe of gardens along the water-side. Towers, churches, and noble-looking edifices mark it as an old city. Around us on all sides are lovely spots—an island here, an islet there, the banks covered with greenest verdure, and the nooks studded with tall tree-ferns. A smart-looking pilot boards us from a cutter, and he steers our good ship close by each point. To our right we have a public garden crowded with gaily-dressed people promenading amidst a wealth of floral beauty—it looks to us a perfect paradise. On the left are innumerable bays and promontories. Between us and the city is a pretty little island bristling with cannon, while lying off are several ships-of-war at anchor flying the British flag, which we salute by dipping our ensign. Our sailors are busily taking in sail, one by one. The pilot shouts—"Starboard!" 'Port!" "Steady!" We pass through a fleet of splendid merchant ships. The helm is put down. The ship is brought head to wind. The anchor is let go. We are in Sydney Harbour—the most beautiful and picturesque in the wide world. Our passengers bid us kindly adieus, and in half-an-hour the ship's company is broken up.

CHAPTER V.

IN COMMAND.

IN good ships sailing from one part of the world to another, I served my time as second mate, then took first mate's certificate, and finally passed as master and got a command.

A young fellow on taking command of a large vessel for the first time has very mixed feelings. He has a certain pride, no doubt, in his position, but the sense of responsibility weighs upon his mind. He is in absolute charge of precious lives and valuable property, and if anything goes wrong he alone will be to blame. It sometimes happens that it is on one's first voyage the greatest trials come.

It was so in my case, at least. I had made a good run out to Java, but on the homeward passage I was caught in a cyclone. We were standing across the variable space which lies between the Island of Java and the Trades. One day we had a succession of squalls, chiefly from SW. About sunset the sky appeared to change for the better, and as far as I could read the indications, a squall we saw coming down on us would probably be lighter and possibly the last. I was mistaken. In a few seconds it came away like fury and struck us with terrific force, rain falling in torrents. We luffed up to it, but heeled over until about at capsizing point. At that moment a huge wave rose to leeward, like a wall, filling the decks fore and aft, and before we had time to recover from the shock, we were taken flat aback by a howling gale from the opposite direction from whence the squall had come. For nearly two hours we continued to make stern-board—one of the most dangerous positions a ship can be placed in with any sea or wind. Every muscle was strained to fill the yards, but all the time the seas ran clear over us from aft, almost knocking the stern in. At length it eased a little and allowed us to square away before it, and soon after with snug canvas we were on our course again.

On going below, to my consternation, I found that during the two brief hours the barometer had fallen over 4-10ths. With the violent sudden change, the fall could mean nothing else but the approach of a cyclone. Fresh from the study of the Law of Storms as I was, it came to be a question how far had I the courage to put confidence in the theoretical teaching of the schools. According to the rules laid down as to the movement of these great circular storms, the cyclone we had got into was coming from the eastward and going to the westward. My first duty was to find out how we stood in relation to its centre. Turning one's back to the wind, we had the centre on the right hand, consequently we were on the left-hand semi-circle or southern edge of the storm. This we knew, because the wind was SE., and the wind in the cyclone in the Southern Hemisphere always turns with the hands of a watch. Having thus satisfied myself theoretically by bearance of the centre, I resolved to scud before the cyclone, and at the same time to steer a little southerly off the course we wished, thus taking advantage of the storm, but gradually moving off its supposed track. For nine days we ran before it in this way, making 220 miles per day, running down ultimately to 150 miles. Each day the gale became stronger, and the sea heavier. Sail after sail had to be taken in. We had a clear ocean before us, and the good ship sped along as fast as the sails would carry her. On the ninth day, however, the race was up. Our enemy which had pursued us so long began to gain rapidly upon us. The whole heavens were black as ink, the wind howled awfully, and the sea was tossed into mountains. The mercury in the barometer sank nearly out of sight, and emitted a bluish flame. One manœuvre alone was left for us, and every possible precaution was taken that it should come right. The bringing of a ship to the wind running before a heavy sea is the most dangerous evolution that can be performed at sea, but I resolved to try it, though the conditions of wind and sea were against us. It was a last chance to save the ship. We could scud in front of the tempest no longer. Barometer, sea, and sky tell us plainly not a moment should be lost. All sails are furled, excepting a lower topsail and a trysail. Now comes the move which is to decide our fate. One roller when the ship is broadside on and the decks may be swept, the hatches burst in, and the masts gone by the board. We expect to founder, but hope to float. Just before the helm is put down, the order is supposed to be given, " Look out for yourselves !" but a trumpet voice could not be heard above the roar of the sea and the howling of the wind. The order is unnecessary, as every one knows the imminent peril of the movement. The helm is put down. The brave little ship comes to grandly. Some spars are carried away, and there was a frightful shock all over, but still we have won. There is a stern joy in defying the tempest and cheating the storm by the handling of one's ship. At the same time the heart involuntarily goes out in gratitude to God for having given us the victory. Before many hours we found the wind hauling to the eastward. Our calculations, based on the scientific theory of the Law of Storms, had proved correct. The cyclone was holding to the westward, while we had been sailing out of its course, and at the same time on the proper tack for heading up to any change in the direction of wind and sea. In short, we had been sailing round the southern verge of the storm until the whole mass had passed us. The cyclone ultimately disappeared below the western horizon. We estimated its diameter at 600 miles, and were truly thankful to have seen the last of it.

A sailor's life is full of incidents. One evening I took a short stroll on shore at Gravesend. We were just about to start on a voyage to Australia, and my vessel, a brand-new three-master, lay off in the stream. I got into conversation with a respectable-looking man who had come out for a walk with his children. I noticed one bright little fellow, and asked the man if he was his eldest son. "That boy," he replied, "is as dear to me as any of my own children, but he is not my son. His father, a ship captain, was drowned at sea, and the mother, a very good woman, who lived next door to us, died soon after, I believe of a broken heart. It was a sad case. I had enough to do to provide for my own family, but I could not help telling the dying woman to keep her mind easy about her son, Tommy. I would bring him up. She just whispered 'God bless you!' and breathed her last. I don't regret it, for Tommy is a good boy, and when he gets a chance I am sure he will do well. He wants to go to sea." I felt interested in the lad, and although I knew it was irregular to have a boy on board whose name was not on the ship's articles, I offered to take him. "Thank you very much, Captain," said his guardian. Tommy's face was radiant with pleasure and pride when half-an-hour later he appeared rigged out, quite smartly, with a blue jacket and white pants, carrying a small canvas bag containing the rest of his belongings. We rowed off to the ship, and I handed Tommy over to the care of the mate, and for the time forgot all about him. I had very soon something else to think about. We proceeded down St. George's Channel, and while standing in for the Welsh coast with the wind ahead, we were suddenly caught by a nor'-wester. Up to that moment the weather had been thick as a hedge, and the breeze strong from the south-west. The barometer had shown no indication whatever of a change. All at once big drops of rain fell, and almost in a moment of time the wind struck us, as I have said, from the north-west. The sky became clear as mid-day, the sea was lashed into foam and spray. Under the change of wind the ship ran straight for the rocks. It was a critical moment for me. Here was a new ship with tall tapering masts whose staying powers had never been tested. Will she come round? I confess I had the gravest apprehensions she would be dismasted by the only manœuvre left to seamanship. I hesitated to give the order. At this moment I became aware of some person at my side, and on looking round I found it was the little boy, Tommy. "Please, Captain," said the little chap, "may I now go below to prayers?" I confess I felt a choking sensation. Here in the midst of a terrible storm was the ship driving to destruction on the rocks, and here was an innocent lad, all unconscious of danger, calmly asking if he might go below to prayers. "Go below this instant, and don't cease praying until I tell you," was my somewhat odd command. The little incident did me good. I could not believe we should be lost while that cabin boy was praying. It nerved me for action. While running before the wind, we had shortened sail, then hauled close to the wind, masts and yards cracking and straining to their utmost tension. All hands were now placed at their stations, and every sailor knew what depended upon him. "Put the helm down!" For a second she shivers and shakes. Everything is strained to the breaking point. We hear the noise of the surf beating against the rocks. It is a moment of dreadful suspense. "She's round! She's round!" shouts every soul on deck. "Let go and haul!" rings cheerily out, and the good ship clears the iron-bound coast and leaves the dangers behind her. When I went below a few minutes later, I found Tommy faithful to the first order he had got from his captain, and told him I hoped he would always have the courage to show his colours as a Christian lad. I have always had the feeling that it was the cabin boy's prayers that saved the ship that night. When the voyage was ended, Tommy went home to Gravesend to his friends. I lost sight of him from that time, and never heard mention of his name. A dozen or more years later, when I was in command of a steamship, then in the London Docks, I observed a particularly smart sailing ship lying outside of us. I had still an eye for a well-kept ship, and I was just remarking to my chief officer that the master of that ship was a proper sailor, when a fine strapping young fellow came on board of us. "You won't remember me, Captain?" he said; "I am the boy Tommy you picked up at Gravesend. I am now master of that sailing ship lying outside of you!" It was a delightful surprise. I afterwards learned that he was held in the highest estimation by the owners he served—one of the best lines of sailing ships out of London. Character tells at sea as much as it does on shore.

For several years I sailed from Glasgow to Java, and thence back to Holland with the produce of the Malay Archipelago. Those were the days of big freights to the shipowner, large profits to the merchant, and handsome gratuities to the captain. In course of time I came to know all the ins and outs of the chain of islands forming the Malay Archipelago. It is always an anxious moment for the master of a vessel when land is first reported. He has been sailing mayhap for three months across the pathless ocean, without having had a single sight of land, and has guided his ship alone by the observations he has made of the sun with his sextant. I confess I always felt a little elated when, bound to Batavia, I made Java Head to a mile, which happened repeatedly.

I have always thought the coral islands of the Java Sea, the most beautiful in the world. Right ahead of us, standing out of the water but a few feet, is one of the reefs shining in the noonday sun, with all the purity of colour of fresh-fallen snow. By and bye, its pearly lustre will be dimmed by the hand of time. Its surface will be covered with mosses and lichen, then will follow a higher order of vegetation, which in turn will be succeeded by the luxurious growths of a tropical clime. You can see islands representing each of these stages of progression. On the older coral islands one can discern the cocoa-nut tree, the plantain, the banana, and the sugar-cane, with a wealth of forest products forming the jungle. The eye detects the different varieties of coral washed by the sea—the white coral with its plant-like shape; the mushroom coral; and the pink and blue coral rising like miniature basaltic columns. Interesting as they are to the naturalist, these coral reefs when coming to the surface are a source of great danger to the navigation of the narrow straits. On the coast of Java, we parcel out the day according to the fixed alternations of the land and sea breezes. We get the sea breeze early in the forenoon, which carries us along until sundown, dying gradually away. Knowing this, we old hands on the coast make the last tack inshore and let go anchor close to the mainland, but with all sails set. It was often very amusing to see some stranger following us in every little dodge to make the most of the wind, but hesitating to copy this last manœuvre. It was a position, however, of perfect safety. Now comes the witching hour of lull. It is impossible to describe the pleasurable sensations one experiences during the brief pause that ensues. The fiery sun has gone down, and everything is hushed in repose. All nature seems at rest, and the cool calm air in which we are now bathed has a wonderfully soothing and refreshing effect. We feel as if transported into a veritable dreamland. To spend the evening watch on this coast is to experience a new sensation in life. It is perfect enchantment. But just as we are at the height of our enjoyment we hear the rustling of the land breeze amongst the trees of the mangrove. The anchor is weighed, and the sails fill with a breeze of perfume. The rich fragrance of the cinnamon, the orange, the sugar cane and other spices, is at first intoxicating, and then becomes almost overpowering, and we are glad to bear away before the breeze.

The hidden coral reefs are not the only source of danger to the navigator amongst these islands. The currents at times are baffling. Coming up on one occasion with a fine ship on her maiden voyage to the Straits of Sunda after a very fast passage, I found dozens of vessels anchored in sheltered nooks in the Strait, where they had been for some weeks, unable to stem the strong current which was running to the south. It so happened that as we approached, a fierce squall called the "Sumatra" came off that shore, and we had the good luck to catch it in the nick of time, and to the surprise of our tide-bound friends who were inshore and could not get underweigh, we headed up through the Strait in the teeth of the current. I knew the Strait pretty well, and although the weather was tempestuous we kept right on, careering through the narrow passage in the darkness of the night, with only the fitful flashes of the lightning to show us the rocks and reefs on the one side, and the hardly less dangerous sands on the other. We got through all right, and I was congratulating myself on this extraordinary piece of good fortune, when the wind died away, leaving us a few miles beyond the mouth of the Strait. Having lost the wind, the way was off the ship, and now to my utter surprise and consternation the current began, gently at first and more rapidly afterwards, to sweep us right back into the Strait again. We tried every method we could think of to retard our course. Anchor we could not—the water was too deep. Backward and backward we were drawn. We felt ourselves completely at the mercy of the treacherous current. Closer and closer it carried us to a small rocky island in the channel. In a few minutes we must be dashed against it. The current was now running like a great river in flood and foam, bearing us along with it. We were within a few hundred yards of the rock, but still there was no slackening in the force. We now waited for the end —the destruction of our good ship. In a moment we were swept in towards the rock, so close that the overhanging branches of the trees brushed our yards. I held my breath for the fatal crash. But it came not. The ship, most mysteriously, stopped short of striking, and remained trembling like a racehorse brought suddenly up in face of an unexpected danger. Here she hung motionless for about five minutes, kept steady apparently by the force of the back draught. All around was the roaring current, and here were we in the very midst of it as steady as if anchored. Gradually she moved round the edge of the island until she had almost made the circle, when her head fell off a little and we shot out into the stream and were once more borne along by the current. On coming into shoal water, we watched our opportunity and let go the anchor, alas! further astern than the friends we had passed so gloriously a few hours before. In the morning the current set the other way and we got through with the others.

Although a sailor's experiences are for the most part connected with the sea, he has occasional curious glimpses of the shore. During the period I was sailing to and from Java, one used to meet at the ports of Batavia and Sourabaya a set of very fine young fellows in command of sailing ships. I believe they were the very pick of the masters in the mercantile service at that time. It was a purely accidental circumstance, I suppose. It would be easy to count a dozen of them at least who became a few years later commanders in the crack steam lines to India and Africa. Long detentions at the Java ports were not unusual, and to break the monotony of harbour life, a party of us arranged to have a short excursion inland, just to see the character of the country whose produce we were carrying to distant shores.

One day a party of us started from Sourabaya to Parsawang by sailing ship. The land all over the Island of Java is low towards the shore, but as a rule there is deep water close up to the beach. It is not so, however, at Parsawang, as we found to our cost. We left the ship by a small native canoe, but had not gone far when it stuck fast. The tide was ebbed or ebbing, and a stretch of shallow water lay between us and the shore. There was nothing for it but off shoes and stockings and wade. We must have presented a comical appearance—each man with his portmanteau and walking-stick trudging through the water for fully a mile. On reaching the shore we were met by a lot of natives, who took charge of our bags. At the first bamboo hut, there was a great stir among them, mustering up tubs of water for our feet, each little fellow sticking close to his patron. A small sum satisfied them, and we were once more comfortable. A little further along we reached the "Boom," or city gate, where we found carriages waiting to drive us to the hotel. An examination of our baggage now took place, and the officer being satisfied, we drove on, the huts becoming thicker as we proceed, and at length the places of the European residents form the line on either side of the road. We spent the evening very comfortably at the hotel, a first rate building, and in the morning started for the famous Blue Waters in an old-fashioned coach drawn by four ponies. The morning drive was delightful. The aroma of the plants and spices still wet with the dew, was exhilarating, and reminded one of the enchanted lands of Eastern romance. Our road led through a bit of country the loveliest in many respects I had ever seen. On one side was the sugar just planted, on the other just reaped, further on half grown, and on the adjacent field were natives burning the refuse of the cane on the land on which it had been grown, brought back from the "fabric" or sugar works. The fertility of the soil is enormous. The coffee plant waves gracefully under the shade of a tree necessary for its proper growth. Close by shoots up the tall Indian corn. Our proximity to a field of maize was always indicated first by the great number of birds. When we came up we found multitudes of the feathered tribe hopping about, some very large birds and few very small, and nearly all exhibiting brilliant colours. We are in the land of the Bird of Paradise, and among birds of the richest plumage in the world. We would fain have spent a few hours here, but the Blue Waters lie a long way ahead of us yet, and the horses are put to their fastest paces once more. The luxurious profusion and growth of vegetation is striking even to those of us who have visited not a few tropical countries. On both sides of the road we were traversing, a great hedge was formed of the natural growth of the country, consisting of the tamarin, cocoa-nut tree, and banyan, whilst in the almost impenetrable underwood grew hundreds of specimens of ferns and flowering plants and shrubs. Through scenery of this character we drove on and reached the Blue Waters, or rather as near as we could approach them with our coach. We had just got out of the old chariot when an incident characteristic of the country occurred. On looking around, we beheld an army of monkeys, emerging out of the forest. There could not have been less than 400 or 500 of them. They were going through a variety of antics, and chattering in the most lively manner. They varied in size from that of a small cat to a pretty large dog, and were quite fat and glossy, presenting a great contrast to the scrubby creatures one sees at home. In the forefront was a large portly leader, who is called the rajah monkey or king by the natives. When a dispute arises between two of his subjects, he immediately runs to the spot, severs the pair of combatants, administering a good thrashing, and distributing to others the disputed property or appropriating it to himself if very dainty. We soon received some attention from them. We had only gone a few hundred yards, when they took possession of our coach. Some of them mounted on top, others with a keen eye to our provisions got on the "boot," while half-a-dozen mischievous rascals rode the horses and began tormenting the poor animals. We had to return to drive them off. Some of them showed fight, and it was with considerable difficulty the native drivers managed to carry our luncheon under cover.

We are now prepared to bathe in the Blue Waters. A house built by the Government stands near the water edge for the use of bathers. The Blue Waters spring from a well, said to be of immense depth, and are allowed to fill up a pond of goodly size, walled in on every side, and reached by a ladder. A sluice carries off the surplus water. A person swimming in this singular bath appears no bigger than a child, and his skin seems perfectly blue. The water feels cold and soft, and is decidedly invigorating, but one is haunted by the fear that one's skin has been rendered permanently blue, and we get out and dress. I observed that the water was of the deepest blue over the crevice through which it rises, but lost much of its bluish tinge when it left the bath. After lunch, we fed the fishes of the Blue Waters with fragments of our provisions. They are very numerous, and are so accustomed to visitors that they will almost feed out of one's hand. The natives hold them sacred, and will on no account catch any of them. Except that they are perfectly blue in colour, they do not differ materially in appearance from common burn trout. We had a stroll round, still escorted by our friends the monkeys, and observed many curious figures in stone, placed about 12 feet apart. The carving was marvellously good, but the representations of human features were very grotesque, and appear to have been made designedly so. In some instances, the teeth were made to project several inches, and not content with giving a man two eyes, some figures were provided with half-a-dozen in front and one or two at the back of his head. Still the sculpture work was remarkably fine. Java abounds with the ruins of ancient temples, and its sculptures rival in beauty those of Central America or even India, but have never been adequately described. The sun now began to make itself felt in its mid-day effulgence, and gathering together our native attendants, we got the old coach underweigh. The monkeys made one or two rallies in force to prevent our departure, but they were beaten off, and we started with them in full cry after us, the old "rajah" shaking his fist when he discovered he was out-distanced in the race.

We returned from Parsawang to Sourabaya by an overland route. The coach horses were changed at stations five or six miles apart along the route. At one station, we were attracted by the sound of music, and on approaching the bamboo huts perceived that some great rejoicings were taking place. We were invited to enter the principal hut, and found ourselves in presence of the "Happy Man," or high priest, of the Javanese. He was celebrating some great feast. The musicians outside were serenading the merry company inside. The band was a curiosity in its way. One man had about a dozen large oblong pieces of metal, mixed with bell-metal, which he beat with a kind of drum-stick, and as each piece gave forth a different tone, the sounds produced were not unpleasant. The other members of the band played seconds to this instrument by striking together two pieces of tin or iron. Though to our ears barbarous as to tune, the music this Javanese band discoursed was not inharmonious, and had a fine effect in the still evening. We spent a short time in, I fear, not very intelligible conversation with the "Happy Man" and his devotees, and then proceeded on our journey.

In our travels along the road, we met the native Rajah of the district. Javanese Royalty still holds a place in the government of the Island, and though no longer supreme in authority the position of the native Rajah is one of some dignity and importance. A handsome salary is allowed him by the Dutch Government, and the Rajah is next in rank to the European Resident. We found that our friend had a handsome palace, and his private grounds, which were enclosed, extended over a space of two miles, beautifully intersected by walks and sheltered by the choicest fruit trees. With great pomp and ceremony he put on his badge of office, and welcomed us to his abode in the most gracious manner, assuring us that his greatest delight was to see Englishmen at his house. He then led the way to a centre table groaning under the choicest viands, and invited us to refresh ourselves. On the floor of the chamber sat his ministers of state, who bowed a welcome, but did not rise. Each of these dusky gentlemen quaffed his glass every time anything important was said or done. His Royal Highness insisted very much that we should remain all night with him in order that we might see his theatricals, which he informed us were performed twice-a-week. This invitation we were reluctantly compelled to decline, but while dinner was being prepared he proposed showing us round the palace. The rooms were all handsomely furnished, the walls hung with costly pictures—in fact everything was quite in European style of the first class. Our inspection was not confined to the principal rooms—he even took us to the cooking department, and at length to the wine cellar, where he drew our attention to his large stock of champagne, of which he seemed rather proud. We returned to the reception room, a large circular apartment, with the roof some forty feet high. The floor was of marble, and from the pillars were suspended large curtains ready to be dropped as soon as the sun shone in upon the floor. In this room was his judgment-seat or throne, lined with dark velvet, trimmed with lace. A servant, his chief butler, now approached the Rajah on his knees and informed him that dinner was ready. We then removed to the dining-hall, his ministers got up off their mats, and took their places on the table at the left, while he most ceremoniously bowed the strangers to his right. He gave us an excellent dinner, the fruits especially being most delicious. At parting we thanked him for his hospitality, and exchanged cards, he giving us besides his own that of his son Dolph, who is Rajah in another district. Our visit to the Rajah formed a very pleasant episode in our journey back to Sourabaya, where we arrived the same evening.

On another occasion I had an unusually long and quite involuntary term of residence on shore. It is the ordinary custom of Dutch skippers when in Java to live on shore. We did not follow their example. Arriving at a small place called Peckalongan, we had to anchor in an exposed bay. One morning I landed and drove up to town, about three miles inland from the entrance, and spent the day on business amongst the European merchants. Returning in the evening to go off to the ship, I found the blue flag was flying, indicating that no boat could cross the bar. The weather had changed—heavy rain falling and a gale of wind blowing, with the usual accompaniment in those parts of thunder and lightning. I could see my ship pitching and rolling not the eighth of a mile from the beach, but to reach her was impossible. I returned to the town and took up my quarters at the hotel, trusting there would soon be a change. Here, however, I had to remain for fourteen days, without getting a single chance of communicating with the ship. For several days the rain was incessant, and the river rose rapidly. On the second day it overflowed its banks, and by the evening it had submerged the town, all except the higher buildings. The scenes presented by the poor natives attempting to save their little property in the midst of the storm were very exciting, though sometimes very amusing. On the fourteenth day I was informed there was a prospect of my getting off to the ship. On going to the harbour I prepared myself for running the bar, but a Dutch friend would not listen to my doing so until I had tried whether it was safe by sending out a crew of natives. I must confess I thought this was rather a cowardly course of procedure, but my friend argued that the chances of escape to them were fifty to one with me. So I let him have his way, and the prudence of his counsel became apparent when it was seen that on reaching the bar the boat capsized and the natives were thrown into the surf. In an instant, however, they got on the boat's keel, and paddling with their feet and hands, brought her back, treating the whole thing as a good joke. An hour or two later I got off, not, however, without finding considerable difficulty in forcing our way through the boiling surf, and I was thankful to have my feet once more on the ship's deck.

A day or two later a deputation of sailors asked for a day on shore. I had some doubts about granting it, as Jack ashore in foreign parts invariably goes in for a lark, which not infrequently ends in a row more or less serious. After lecturing them a bit on the propriety of good behaviour, one watch was allowed on shore for the day. They were not very long in the town until they indulged in all sorts of diversions, riding on horses and driving furiously through the streets. Having summarily got rid of the native drivers, Jack was in full possession of box and whip. Nothing more serious than the upsetting of two or three coaches into a ditch occurred, until the evening, when I received an official intimation from the Resident, or chief representative of the Dutch Government, that my sailors had taken the town and were disregarding all law and order. I had to go after them, and after a good deal of persuasion and a little compulsion I got them to go on board, to the great relief of the inhabitants. I had made up my mind to grant no more liberty days, but unfortunately my order to that effect did not reach the ship until the other watch had left. All I could do was to impose severer injunctions upon this lot, and I was gratified to find them returning to town in the afternoon after a drive into the country, in a thoroughly respectable condition. I saw them off in their boats without, as I thought, any mischief occurring this time. In the evening, however, to my no small astonishment, I was besieged at the hotel by a host of excited natives, presenting bills for payment of such things as young dogs, monkeys, parrots, ducklings, cats, and all manner of fowls which they alleged had been taken by my sailors. It turned out that the second lot was as bad as the first, for on going down the river, wishing to wind up the day with a little exciting sport, they had landed at a village and had literally robbed the place of every living animal they could lay hold on. On going aboard I found the decks presenting the appearance of a small menagerie. Jack, however riotously inclined, is not generally dishonest, and they were perfectly willing that I should settle with the natives for them, which I did to the last farthing.

CHAPTER VI.

STEAMSHIPS.

My last sailing ship was named the " County of Nairn," my native shire. One becomes excessively fond of a good ship which has borne you along in safety through many a stormy sea. A sailor can never believe but that his ship is an intelligent creature, full of life and spirit, willing to do his utmost for him under his direction. I had sailed the " County of Nairn" for a good many years, making many a prosperous voyage with her. She was one of the smartest sailing vessels of the time. It was therefore with some regret that I learned that I was to be removed from command of her. I could not complain, however, as it was in the way of very considerable promotion. I was to get the command of a large steamer being built on the Clyde—the pioneer of a projected line of steamers to Java. I had some right to regard the appointment as a mark of confidence in me, as I knew nothing whatever of steamships. All my experience had hitherto been in sailing vessels. All shipmasters regard steamer captains as decidedly inferior to them as sailors. Without saying how far I shared this prejudice, I thought if I could manage a ship under sail I could navigate a vessel under steam, and accordingly I did not hesitate to accept the command of the steamship "County of Sutherland."

Standing on the bridge of this magnificent steamer of 3000 tons, as we proceeded down the Clyde on the trial trip, I could not help recalling my first voyage in the little smack "Mary," and wondering what my dear old mother thought of it all now. The change from the one class of vessel to the other is really a complete revolution in a sailor's experience. In the case of the captain, he finds fresh demands on his capacity to command and new calls on his intelligence and resources. The knowledge acquired on board a sailing vessel is not lost, but it has to be applied to a different set of circumstances. In the case of the steamer, there is the sense of power; in that of the sailing ship, the knowledge of tactics. But the work of navigation is practically the same in both.

Leaving or approaching any of the leading ports of Great Britain is like driving through the crowded streets of a great city. The scene which the English Channel presents on a fine clear night has often struck me as exceedingly beautiful. On the French side the coast, as we proceed down, is lighted all along with the regularity of a leading street in the metropolis, only for lamps you have magnificent lighthouses casting their bright gleams athwart the dark heaving ocean, one guiding you by its grateful light until you have caught sight of the upward shaft of the next. On the English side you have a less regular system of lighthouses, but scarcely less effective. We have just lost sight of the Nore lightship when we see, twenty-five or thirty miles ahead, the two brilliant triangular lights of the Foreland, the one high up on the summit of the chalk cliff, the other in a position lower down. Here you may sail close in to the perpendicular cliff until its shadow shuts out the blazing lights overhead;—then stand off. Having once more got the rays of light to fall on the deck, the mariner now sees, like so many twinkling stars, the lights on the Goodwin Sands, and as he approaches them, they seem to illuminate the heavens. A little ahead is the Varne lightship, flashing out its red gleams, and on the other side are the variegated lights of Dover Pier and Ramsgate, with the brilliant electric light of Dungenness in the distance. The Sovereign Shoal, long one of the terrors of the English Channel, has now its lightship to warn of danger, and next we have the powerful revolving light of Beachy Head, standing about 300 feet above the level of the sea. From this point we have a succession of lights until we reach the famous Eddystone Lighthouse, and one light after another until we take leave of the English Channel.

But it is not for the benefit of our solitary vessel that these lights shine. This lighted ocean pathway teems with shipping. Steamers of every size and of every nation are passing up and down. Fleets of vessels are coming up full sail with a favourable breeze. Vessels going down are tacking hither and thither, and mixed up with them are the fishing boats with a bright torchlight burning fiercely at the masthead. With all these innumerable craft, with white, red, and green lights dancing, as it were, on the face of the water, the Channel presents a picture of marvellous animation and interest. But this of course is not the constant appearance it presents. The English Channel is the most difficult part to navigate in a voyage round the world. Channel weather is proverbially bad, and instead of the well-lighted coast to guide us, we are often left to grope our way in the densest darkness and stormiest weather. The fog has descended, and extinguished as far as we are concerned every light and landmark. Our progress down Channel then becomes an ordeal. The speed is eased, the lookout is doubled, the steam whistle is kept going. A fierce, cold wind dashes rain, hail, and spray from the sea into your eyes. The lookout shouts—"A green light on the port bow!" We put the helm hard a-starboard. No sooner done than the cry is—"A red light on the starboard bow!" and then a moment later —"A bright light close-to, right ahead!" The order is then—"Hard-a-port, slow, stop her, go astern." While we are thus endeavouring to steer clear of passing vessels, we are at the same time anxiously trying to ascertain our position by the lead. The leadsman's song, as he heaves the leadline in the cold frosty water, is—"By the deep 8,"—"by the mark 5,"—"and a quarter 4!" We are close upon a shoal, and the order is instantly given for altering the course into deeper water.

If we substitute for the fog, thick drizzling rain and a furious gale, and if, instead of going down Channel, we are coming in from the South without having got sights for several days or seen any vestige of land, with compasses indicating incorrectly and chronometers doubtfully reliable, then the navigation of the English Channel, with all its dangers of collisions, rocks and shoals, becomes a thousandfold more difficult. The wonder often is not how many but how few vessels have made shipwreck in such circumstances. On such nights, the highest seamanship is required to navigate the English Channel.

To make a voyage to Java by steamer, I found was very much more comfortable than by sailing ship. My knowledge of the Java coast enabled me to cut off many a corner as we steamed in and out of the narrow channels. As the pioneer vessel of a new enterprise, one had to encounter a host of unexpected difficulties. The great drawback was the want of despatch from the shore at the smaller ports, the necessary organisation not having got into working order. After we had made a few voyages, the Dutch merchants became alarmed lest the carrying trade should pass entirely out of their hands, and they decided to start an opposition steam line, to be subsidised by the Dutch Government. The sugar trade also at this time began its downward tendency, ending a year or two later in a collapse. It was therefore deemed advisable not to proceed with our intended line of steamers, and eventually my steamer, the "County of

Sutherland," was withdrawn and put into the East Indian trade. I had now the opportunity of making an acquaintance with the Mediterranean ports and the Suez Canal route to India, with occasional diversions to other parts of the world.

One of the most interesting voyages I made was through the Dardanelles and the Bosphorus in the spring of 1878. It was a time of great political excitement. An armistice between Russia and Turkey had been effected, and the representatives of the Great Powers were assembled at Berlin. The passage at any time from Genoa to the Black Sea, a distance of nearly seventeen hundred miles, is a very attractive one; on this occasion there was the additional interest of war excitement.

On leaving Genoa, the first place of interest on the way is Monte Cristo, where the prisoner of the Chateau d'Iff found a home. Not many hours' distant is the volcanic island of Stromboli. It was daytime when we passed, but the smoke and fire belching forth and the lava rolling down the face of the island into the sea were distinctly visible. This occurs on the north-west side, for immediately behind the smoking chasm is a precipitous mountain which Nature has seemingly formed for the protection of all the other parts. Vegetation thrives in a wonderful degree; everything is green and luxuriant. The sides of the hill are terraced and cultivated to nearly the summit, and there are two thriving little towns, one on each side, the inhabitants of which live on the produce of the volcanic island. We passed within half-a-mile, and saw an English gentleman—we judged him to be so from his dress—whiling away an hour fishing in a little boat. Otherwise, for all we saw of them, though it was noon, the inhabitants might have been asleep.

A few hours later we were sailing through the Straits of Messina—a truly lovely passage. On both sides the hills are cultivated in terraces, with orange groves, vines and figtrees—the fruit hanging temptingly almost before our eyes. The inhabitants here seemed all alive, and appeared to have made a point of coming out to see us pass. The Straits are about a mile wide, with a fearfully rapid current rushing to the north, indeed so strong was it that several times it took complete charge of the ship. A few days' open sea sailing, and we were amongst the classic Isles of Greece. They are by no means high, nor truth to tell very attractive, many of them being apparently barren, but their strange configuration and the singular winding passages between them, along with their ancient history, invest them with peculiar interest. The entrance to the Bay of Naples and the Temple of Neptune is exceedingly fine. Passing Origo and Diro, we steered for the island of Metylene, thence to Tenedos. We passed two vessels of the British Fleet lying in Besika Bay, and arrived at the entrance to the Dardanelles. On either side is a fort, which seemed to me formidable enough to stand any assault, if defended with pluck and skill. Whether they would bar the entrance against the fire of such ships as the "Devastation" and the "Temairare," I would not venture to say. The position they occupy appears to be impregnable against any ordinary assault. With the exception of a small garrison town on each side, there is nothing worthy of remark along the Dardanelles. The banks are very steep, and there is a conspicuous want of agriculture. The passage is about four miles wide until we come to Chanak. Here all ships bound up, under penalty of being fired at, have to stop and send a bill of health ashore and receive official permission to proceed. A few more turns round corners and we are at Gallipoli, where we salute five of Her Majesty's ships of war lying under the fort guns. The fort wears a very neglected appearance, and does not look to be a strong place of arms. In the space of three hours from entering the Dardanelles we were in the Sea of Marmora, distant about 120 miles from Constantinople. We pass Cape Stefano about 10 p.m., and could hear distinctly the Russian drums and bugles sounding. Passing close to the old Seraglio Point, whereon stood the palace burned down a few years ago—it is supposed, by one of the Sultan's many wives—we soon arrive at Constantinople, or the entrance to the Golden Horn, where we anchor.

We were up at sunrise, and saw what certainly appeared to us the finest city in the world. I have seen most places of note approachable by ship, but the view of Constantinople from the sea is the grandest of all. On the Asiatic side are numerous mansions, surrounded with beautiful gardens, the vines trellised to the edge of the shore. On the west side is an arm of the sea crowded with ships of every nation. The scene on the water is animated and picturesque beyond description, while right in front rise up palaces innumerable, with their domes, towers, turrets and minarets glittering in the early sunshine with a golden radiance. The magnificence of the buildings as seen from the bay, gives the beholder an impression of dazzling beauty and oriental splendour.

No less than twenty-one steamers arrived here in one day. All vessels bound through the Bosphorus must anchor and pay toll of nearly £2 per hundred tons register. This little matter took several hours to accomplish, as besides the Turkish officials, the Russian and British Consuls have to sign our documents. During the few hours I had to spare, I had a ramble through the part of the city nearest the water, and my vision of oriental splendour speedily vanished—narrow, dirty streets, paved with boulders laid down haphazard, dung heaps and scores of mangy dogs lying upon them —everything dirty and disgusting, and the dwellers a very mixed lot. Types of every nationality in the world were to be met with. I would not willingly pass through one of these streets at night. My friend told me, however, not to judge of Constantinople from the part I had seen. The news had just come that the British Government had ordered native troops from India, and doubt and uncertainty existed among all the business men. What puzzled all of them was the fraternal feeling which had sprung up between the Turkish Court and the Russian officers.

I lost no time in getting my papers. The Turkish officials informed me that the two leading lights for the entrance of the Bosphorus had been extinguished for the present, while the English Consul gave me official warning on no account to attempt to enter Odessa harbour without the steam-launch pilot stationed outside for the purpose of guiding ships clear of torpedoes—rather a lively prospect certainly. However, we clear, and steam boldly up the Bosphorus. It is a very charming and picturesque waterway, with splendid mansions and terraced gardens almost the whole way up. The passage is narrow, barely a mile wide, with a strong current running westward. Once more we had to land with our papers for examination, and we then cleared for the Black Sea.

We arrived off Odessa at 10 p.m. (22nd April). Within two miles of the port, not a twinkle of a leading light of any kind was visible—a few street and house lights alone were to be seen. Thinking we might find something to guide us, I steered for where I thought the harbour must be, but we had not gone far when we were warned off by a succession of danger signals flashed from the Russian guardship lying about a mile and a half south of the entrance. We lost no time in hauling off, and now steered straight for the ship which had shown the lights. Not being able to communicate by night, we anchored close to her, and waited daybreak. As soon as it was clear, we made the usual preparations for getting underweigh, but were stopped by a signal from the guardship—" Don't try to enter without a pilot." We immediately hoisted—" Can a pilot be got?" The answer was—" Wait till he comes." By this time a Russian transport arrived with invalids from Constantinople, and being in the service and secrets of the Government, knew what to do. After exchanging signals with the guardship, she made a few serpentine turns, and proceeded on. The Austrian mail came up, and was stopped by the same signal as we had been. In the course of a few hours a small paddle steamer came out of the harbour, and when close to hoisted the signal—" I have a pilot, follow me." We did so as nearly as possible, making several turns. After passing first a black buoy and then a red one, he left us to steer for the harbour ourselves. I had an idea that all this mystery was just a bit of humbug. From the circuitous route we were obliged to take, I concluded the torpedoes were laid down as thick as possible right in front of the entrance at about half-a-mile distance, and our turnings and twistings round supposed dangers outside were simply performed to mislead us as to the true position of the torpedoes, which were to the north of us, marked by the black buoy. At the time, I felt I would not have hesitated to have gone in if necessary without our friend of the paddle steamer, and a few days later I received information from a reliable source that the torpedoes were laid down abreast of the town in four lines, running parallel with the coast and only a few yards apart, and numbered in all about four hundred. They constitute the real defence of Odessa, for the forts are not formidable by any means. The Russian soldiers have not the smart, tidy appearance of our men. They seem always dirty, and their uniforms bespattered with mud and grease, no doubt the effect of being so much employed as labourers. The officers, however, are very handsome fellows, especially those connected with the staff of some prominent general. There was no enthusiasm for war among the populace, but rather a gloomy foreboding of being called anew to face a great calamity. The ardour of the military spirit may well have been depressed for the moment by the sad spectacle of the arrival of ship after ship full of sick and wounded soldiers from the scene of the war, temporarily suspended.

All the talk in Odessa was about the action of the British Government in bringing the Indian troops to Malta. It had produced something like a scare, and an amusing incident occurred in connection with the state of feeling, for which I was accountable. On the afternoon of the second day after our arrival, the sarang, or headman, of my crew of Lascars, asked permission for himself and his men to go on shore for a stroll. These Indian natives are full of harmless vanity, and their object in going ashore was not to see the wonders of Odessa, but to be seen. They like nothing better than to be stared at. As there was no harm in gratifying them, I allowed them to go on shore, not dreaming that the Russian authorities would have any objection, though, to be sure, I had on arrival signed a formal declaration that no one was to leave the ship while in port, except myself, without special permission asked and obtained. Away some forty of these fellows went up town, marching three and three in regular procession. No sooner did they make their appearance on the main streets than they struck perfect terror in the breasts of the Russians. The police fled, and the people on the streets took refuge in shops and houses. All the time our Indian friends, with perfect gravity and unconcern, were airing themselves in front of the principal buildings. Presently a detachment of soldiers was brought down from the citadel, and after various strategical manœuvres, made a rush upon the harmless natives, calling upon them (in Russian) to lay down their arms. Of course the poor souls offered no resistance, though they kept shouting that they belonged to the "County of Sutherland" (meaning the steamer of that name) and were doing no wrong. The brave Russian soldiers, however, made prisoners of war of them, and sent them to prison. In the evening I got the British Consul to induce the Governor of Odessa to let them out, but only after repeated declarations that they were sailors, not soldiers or a contingent of Malta troops. When I went for them to prison they were crying like children. Now if they had been English sailors who had been interfered with in this way, they would have had something to say to the Russian police before they would have been content to be locked up. However, it was better as it was, and in justice to the Indians I should mention that some time after they got on board, a deputation of them, armed with heavy sticks, came to me with the request that they should be allowed to go on shore to thrash the Russian police for having insulted the subjects of the Empress of India. Not having been empowered by Lord Beaconsfield to declare war against Russia, and not caring to do so on my own account, I reluctantly refused them permission.

A day or two later I had a visit from his Excellency the Governor of Odessa, Count Lobanoff, and showed him over the ship, in which he appeared much interested. I had a couple of fine orchids in the cabin which he greatly admired, one of which I presented to him. He said he had, like one of our English statesmen, a great passion for orchids, but could not often indulge his taste for them. We had some talk about the practicability of using merchant vessels in time of war. The Russians are not allowed to have a fleet on the Black Sea, but they have a very strong line of merchant steamers, which could be turned into transports and war ships. None of them, however, came up to our tonnage. We were the largest merchant steamer they had seen at Odessa, and our quick run from the Bosphorus had excited much interest. A host of military and naval officials visited us, amongst others the captain of one of the two Popendoff circular warships which lay in the harbour, with whom I had a very pleasant conversation. The drift of all their enquiries was whether it was not possible to build a type of steamer suitable for trade in time of peace, and readily adaptable for naval purposes in time of war.

The intelligence from London being far from re-assuring as to peace, we hurried up our loading of wheat as much as possible. There were thirty English steamers taking in grain—wheat and barley for England and France, and rye for Holland. The grain was of a very poor quality, but I suppose the price to the merchant corresponded with its value. On leaving Odessa we were again led out clear of the torpedoes. We spent Sunday at Constantinople, and visited Pera, the fashionable quarter. The impression I formed on my first visit remained. Constantinople is the grandest capital in the world, its population the vilest on earth.

CHAPTER VII.

THE OCEAN HIGHWAY.

The types of character one meets on board a passenger steamer between England and India are extremely varied. Passengers as a rule endeavour to be on pleasant terms with the captain, and one forms many agreeable acquaintanceships and some lasting friendships.

On one occasion I had a gentleman from Glasgow, of the name, I shall say, of Black. Along with Mr Black was Miss Sarah Parker, a lady of considerable notoriety. Both were going out to join the Theosophists under Madame Blavatzki, at Madras. Sarah Parker had played many a *role* in her day. She had met Madame Blavatzki in America when lecturing on spiritualism, and so impressed was the latter with her talents that she repeatedly urged her to come out to India. Miss Sarah had accepted the invitation, and was now on her way to Madras. She was in charge of Mr Black, if a lady of her mature experience could be said to be under the protection of any one. Though they were co-religionists they did not get on particularly well, and before half the voyage was accomplished, they were not on speaking terms. Mr Black was rich and had paid

Miss Sarah Parker's passage out. The relation of patron and patronised is not a very happy basis of friendship, and in this case did not stand the strain of a sea voyage. Black was a fine young fellow, but full of strange notions and ideas. His father had recently died, and he had come in for a considerable fortune. His mind had been turned to thoughts of religion, and of all the systems he knew theosophy promised him the best solution of his difficulties. He had studied Theosophy in London under Mr Cinnet, author of the "Occult Sciences," and had determined to devote his wealth to the propagation of the cause in India. He had met Miss Sarah Parker at Mr Cinnet's. In the evenings he and I had often long serious talks together. Brought up as I had been on the Shorter Catechism, my views naturally did not run on the same lines as his. As a sailor I had come to adopt as a working creed—"Trust in God and do the right." I reasoned with him as to the folly of supposing that the Almighty would make use of such mediums as those he knew for the purpose of special revelations. He admitted readily enough that our dear shipmate Dr Sarah Parker was not an angel or a very spiritual medium, but he always wound up by saying if I only knew Madame Blavatzki I would change my opinion. "Look here, Mr Black," I used to say, "you will find out when it is perhaps too late that the whole thing is a fraud and Madame Blavatzki an impostor." He was not convinced. What my arguments failed to do, a nice young English girl very nearly accomplished. Mr Black fell in love with the young lady. For some time I think it hung in the balance whether it was to be the sweet lassie and marriage or Madame Blavatzki and Theosophy. Mr Black had to make his choice speedily, as the young lady and her mother and sisters were going on to Calcutta. He was booked only to Madras. Miss Sarah Parker and I were the best of friends. She is undoubtedly clever, and as she knew I did not believe in her spiritualism and spirit-rapping she did not bother me.

My connection with the Theosophists did not cease on arrival at Madras. Next day I accepted an invitation to luncheon at Madame Blavatzki's retreat at Adyar, a sweet little spot a short distance from Madras. Mr Black was there and so was Miss Sarah. Madame Blavatzki impressed me greatly. I could quite understand how a woman of her character could acquire influence over certain types of mind. Her bearing was most distinguished, and in her presence one could believe that she was a Russian Princess, which she claimed to be. She was most gracious to me, and told me that she knew of all that had been going on on board of my vessel from the communications from the unseen spiritual world she had been receiving. She mentioned some little incidents—I knew perfectly that the gossip had been retailed to her by Sarah. Black looked astonished, as if he was listening to wonderful revelations. A Frenchman and his wife, of the name of Coulomb, also were at lunch. I did not take to them. Madame Coulomb took part in laying out the lunch, and then sat down with the guests. On rising from the table for a stroll in the garden, Madame Blavatzki detained me for a little, and asked me if I would like to see some of her manifestations with the spirits. She performed some little tricks in a cabinet, mere sleight-of-hand exhibitions. I was much less impressed by them than I was by her intellectual powers. The conclusion I came to was that Madame Blavatzki was a woman of remarkable ability, who had taken up this Theosophy business as a means of livelihood, and that the whole thing was a fraud. The pity is that in India their dupes can be counted by tens of thousands. We parted. Mr Black remained behind in Madras, and threw in his lot with the Theosophists. Madame Blavatzki's influence over him was greater than that of his winsome shipmate, who went on with us to Calcutta. I could not help thinking he would have been a happier man if he had followed the dictates of natural affection and let Theosophy slide.

Individual idiosyncracies soon show themselves at sea. We had Colonel Bryne of aeronaut fame as a passenger home on one occasion. Passing Point de Galle, we were signalling to the flag staff on shore simply our number, consisting of four square flags in one hoist. Seeing us preparing to hoist the flags, the Colonel came along, and asked quite seriously if I would kindly let them know on shore that he was on board! I demurred somewhat—it would occupy too long a time in spelling out a communication of that kind, and I would require to stop the ship. "Nonsense!" he replied; "you can do it in two hoists." Taking up the code of signals with the familiarity of an old hand, he pointed out the word "Brine" on one page, and "on board" on another. These two signals which read "Brine on board!" were hoisted up. The answer we got back from the shore was —"Thanks, got plenty pickle!" Such is fame. The Colonel looked daggers at the signal station, and declared that he would make these fellows smart for it. I believe he reported them at the Colonial office as a most inefficient staff.

A drinking man on board a passenger ship is a great nuisance. We had a very bad case on a voyage home from India. He joined the ship a hopeless drunkard— he left it a confirmed teetotaller. Mr Smith bore a sad reputation in India. He was sent home by his friends, who charged me to give him no liquor. It is easier to make a stipulation of this kind than to carry it out. We had very bad weather at the start, and I had something else to do than dry-nurse a dissipated passenger. When the weather improved a bit, however, I enquired of the chief steward how Smith was regulating his drinking habits, and regretted to learn that his consumption of liquor was outrageous. I considered it to be my duty to stop the supply. After dinner that day, Smith's bottle having run dry, he asked the steward for another bottle, but was informed that I had given instructions to stop his liquor. He was very indignant, and intimated his intention of interviewing me on the subject. The ship at the time he approached me was rolling a good deal, and I wondered not a little how Smith managed to get along to the skylight on the upper deck where I was. "Would you speak a minute, please," he said. "Certainly," I replied; and as it was still unsafe for any one to stand on deck, let alone my friend Smith, I asked him to step into the chart-room. "Well, Smith," said I, "what is it you want?" "Have you stopped my grog?" he asked. "I have," I replied. "Then I should like to know why," he rejoined. "Because," said I, "you have been drinking too much, and if you were allowed to continue it at the same rate you would be a dead man long before we reached London." Warming up a bit, I said—"Look here, Smith, let us understand each other. I am responsible for your conduct on board this boat so far as drink is concerned, and have fully resolved to make you a total abstainer. You are one of those men who should avoid drink as you would the bite of a snake." The scornful look he gave me I shall never forget. However, instead of giving vent to his angry feelings in abuse, he began very skilfully to involve me in an argument. He asked whether I considered it right that he should be made a teetotaller without having the credit of the effort and resolution required to attain this end. "There is no man alive," he said, "who is more anxious than I am for reformation in respect of drink, but my objection now is, not to the attempt to bring it about, but to the method by which you propose accomplishing the change. Suppose now that instead of suddenly stopping the supply, you instructed the steward to let me have another bottle, I will promise to hang it up in my room (after having taken a small drop), and every time I go in I will point my finger to it and say 'There you are, but I won't touch you.' In this way I shall have some credit in the transaction." Having been somewhat impressed by Smith's seriousness of manner, I said—" Now, my friend, give me your word of honour that you will do as you have suggested and I will order another bottle at once!" Smith grasped my hand in token of the bargain, and left the chart-room to go below. The ship was still rolling very heavily—Smith stumbled and fell head first on to the middle platform of the staircase. It was a mere chance he was not washed overboard. I resolved to fall back on my first resolution, and instructed the doctor to serve him only with medicinal quantities. When Smith was informed of the arrangement by the doctor, he got into a towering passion. "Do you think I came on board this ship to be insulted either by the Captain or you? Take your liquor away!" From that hour he became a total abstainer—never asked for or touched a drop of liquor all the time he was on board, and I believe has kept a perfectly steady man ever since. We had awakened a latent feeling of self-respect and made a new man of him.

I had the luck to be assigned the leading part in several public demonstrations. In the year 1879 I was lying at Havre, when instructions came to proceed to

Newport, Mon., in order that my ship might open the new dock there. We had a splendid reception— bands playing, banners flying, and crowds cheering. Our passage up the river was something like a royal progress. The ceremony of entering the new dock was successfully accomplished by " the big ship," as the good people of Newport were pleased to call us. Newport and the adjacent country were *en fete*. Thousands of visitors inspected us. She was the largest vessel the country people had ever seen, and her saloon, engines, and steering gear excited the utmost interest. I was going up town one day in a little omnibus, and the whole subject of talk among my fellow passengers was the big steamer. " Have you been on board ?" said one countryman to another. " Yes, and saw everything. It is just wonderful." " Yes," said the other, " it is just a floating palace. What a clever man the captain of a ship like that must be!" "That's just what I have been thinking. I would have given something to have seen him, but he wasn't on board. I am told he is a Scotchman." " A Scotchman, is he !" exclaimed the other; " that accounts for it all. The Scotch and Welsh are just like brothers. My wife is Scotch, and she'll be very proud when I tell her that!" After all, it is only a very small proportion of the population who ever see a large ocean steamer, and I am satisfied were some of the great passenger lines to send an occasional steamer to the remoter parts of the United Kingdom, they would find the advantage of it in an increased number of passengers. It is really the dread of the dangers of the sea which keeps the country people from emigrating.

When the harbour improvements at Capetown in South Africa were inaugurated, I had the honour of being the first to enter with a large steamer, and great were the congratulations and rejoicings. I shall never forget a little incident which happened to me on that coast. We loaded in Table Bay, and one beautiful evening hove up our anchor, turned round and steamed to sea bound for Algoa Bay. Table Mountain wore the usual grey hood of flying cloud, but otherwise, as I described it in the deck log, "the night was clear and fine, sea smooth, thermometer 68 deg." A few minutes before leaving we had finished taking in 150 tons of dynamite, transhipped from a steamer bound for Australia. We had also a number of pine logs on deck, secured with rope and chain lashings. After sighting the lighthouse which stands on the southern point of Africa, I went below to sleep, tired after a hard day's work. At midnight, just four hours after we had started, I was awakened by the noise of wind and hail, and getting on deck found we had just been struck by a hurricane. The sea in less than an hour ran mountain high, and when on top of one of these huge rollers the starboard wheel-chain was carried away, and we broached to, the sea filling the deck from stem to stern. At the same time the logs got loose from their fastenings, and smashed up bulwark stanchions and everything they came in contact with. Somehow we managed to repair the broken chain, and hove to until daylight. On opening the hatches, we found that some twenty cases of dynamite had been pitched from the upper deck into the lower hold!

We had great celebrations with the steamship "Clan Macintosh" on her maiden voyage in September, 1883. She is a vessel of about 4000 tons, and was fitted up with all the latest improvements up to date. It was part of my business to popularise the new ship, and to entertain as largely as I saw fit. It happened that we carried the first cargo of piece goods under a new contract of the Bombay Native Merchants' Association, and a great stir was created amongst the native merchants by our arrival. To celebrate the event, a native theatrical performance was given on board. We were grandly illuminated. The stage was erected at the forecastle, and the Parsee Opera Company delighted the natives with their performance. During the proceedings, the Chairman of the Association made a congratulatory speech, and concluded by presenting me with a silver cup as a memento of the happy occasion. Such events break the monotony which is apt to prevail in the regular routine on board a liner.

CHAPTER VIII.

IN THE TRANSPORT SERVICE.

The part which our first-class merchant steamers will probably play in the exigencies of a great war is a subject of considerable public interest. My little experience in the transport service may be regarded as a practical experiment.

In 1882, my steamer was chartered by the Indian Government for the conveyance of Indian troops to the Egyptian War, and I had the honour of carrying the 2nd Belooches, some 750 strong, from Karachi to Ismalia.

The harbour of Karachi is a very fine one, and encloses about half-a-dozen miles of smooth water. It probably never looked better or gayer than it did the morning we embarked our men and mules. Of the latter we had 280, chiefly intended for the transport of baggage. Europeans and natives in thousands were afloat early to bid us farewell. The appearance of the Belooches on the Mereweather Pier, as they stood with their arms at the order, just as the sun rose that morning, was as pretty a sight as I had ever seen. In their blue tunics and red breeches they made a grand picture.

Long before noon, every man and mule were in their places, baggage stowed away, and the officers waiting for the final inspection of the Brigadier-General. He came, and having gone the round of the ship, expressed his gratification at the smart and orderly manner in which they had embarked. Just as he was about to bid us farewell, a party of the officers of the law stepped on board, and in the Queen's name served us with arrests for the detention of nearly half the regiment. Every one from the Brigadier-General downwards appeared nonplussed, perplexed, disappointed. The Belooches, we learned from the officers of the law, some time previous to this had been stationed at Karachi for a year or so, and considered that they had been cheated by the bazaar merchants who supplied their provisions—the discovery of the alleged roguery practised upon them being made only the night before they received orders to march up country. They had not forgotten the butchers and bakers of Karachi—indeed, they appear to have been nursing their wrath against them, and looked upon the troubles in Egypt as a providential interference, whereby they could pay off old scores against their enemies. Accordingly about 300 of them asked and obtained leave the previous evening to visit the bazaar on the pretence of buying a few necessaries for their journey. Reaching the bazaar, they found their victims, all unconscious of approaching danger, sitting humbly at the receipt of custom. The Belooches made a furious attack upon them, and the bazaar became a scene of violent disorder. The result of it all was that some thirty of the bazaar merchants had to be carried to hospital, and the Belooches made off with enormous booty, amply sufficient to cover any former losses which they had unjustly sustained at the bazaar.

After a brief consultation by the Brigadier-General, the Lieutenant-Governor of Bengal and myself, the following resolution was formally adopted—"That the officers of justice having duly performed their duty, be informed that as the Regiment is under sailing orders for the seat of the war in Egypt, no civil process can be recognised!"

The Belooches were once more free! The band struck up "Should auld acquaintance be forgot!" (a little ironically in the circumstances) and in a few minutes we were steaming gaily down the harbour. We were nearing the pier head; the pilot had just left us, and the band was playing "My love she's but a lassie yet!" I gave the order full steam ahead. Three minutes later we were struck by a heavy beam sea, and were going right in the teeth of a furious gale. (The S.W. monsoon was at its height.) It was amusing to see the effect on the gallant warriors. Every instrument in the band seemed to choke in the middle of a note. The sweet sounds terminated abruptly, and the bandsmen, most of them afloat for the first time, lay where they fell. The English officer whose duty it was to go the round of the sentries, for several days had to report finding the guards over open hatches and powder magazines in serious default—they were discovered time after time lying behind a spar, unable to stand. In short, the 2nd Regiment of Beloochees had collapsed. I must say, however, the weather was exceedingly rough, and continued so for some eight days, but there was nothing for it but to go ahead full speed across the Arabian Sea. Our cook-houses were on deck, but no fires were lit for over a week. The cooks could not be found, but I really think there was not a single request or desire for warm food all the time. A handful of dry rice and a mouthful of water sufficed for the keenest appetites amongst them. In fact the great majority of them were helplessly ill. With the advent of fine weather, however, they swarmed like bees, and the blue smoke curled once more from the neglected cooking depôts. The cooks were found, and double rations dispensed all round. The bandsmen, recovered and refreshed, polished their instruments, and gave us two hours of excellent music each evening. The change was a pleasant one to all of us, and during the passage up the Red Sea we began to prepare our arms and to anticipate the glorious victories that awaited the Indian Contingent in the Egyptian desert.

After a run of twelve and a half days from Karachi, we arrived at Suez and were ordered into dock to disembark, which we set about as smartly as possible. Suez dock is a very commodious place, and is provided with every facility for dispatch. Our troops walked ashore with their accoutrements and baggage, ready for the campaign. As to the mules, they were perfectly astonished and overjoyed at the sudden change from the heated hold to the free air of the wharf, and expressed their delight by kicking out in all directions. They afforded great fun to the sailors. Jack is never happier than when among horses, mules, and donkeys, though there is nothing he knows less about than how to manage them. Next morning we received orders to re-embark our troops again, and proceed with all despatch to Ismalia. We immediately carried out our instructions, and set about protecting our engine-room and other vulnerable parts of the ship with iron plates. We sailed the same day, and arrived at Ismalia the following afternoon, anchoring close inshore. After reporting our arrival at head-quarters, we were ordered to disembark the troops, the Belooches in small steamers, and the mules, ten at a time, in a punt. The men landed all right, and could have lost no time in forming and marching to their quarters, as I dined with them under canvas that same evening. The mules, perhaps dreading another order to embark, after pawing the sand for an hour or two, made a general stampede, and were with difficulty collected by a sort of prairie hunt amongst the tents of the Guards and the Seaforth Highlanders.

One of the first Field Officers I met was General Herbert Macpherson, who was in command of the Indian Contingent. He had arrived on board the "Tenasserim." General Macpherson hailed from the same part of the country as I did. He left the Nairn

Academy about the time I went to school, but the story of his having fired a small cannon in the playground and brought down a large piece of the wall, to the terror and alarm of the lieges, was often spoken of among the smaller boys, of which I was one. It was in consequence of that little incident that he left school. The town authorities took a serious view of the affair, and Herbert Macpherson was summoned to appear at the police court. His father thought it was time Herbert was engaged in business, and sent him to London to a merchant's office. Learning that the 78th Highlanders had been decimated by cholera, he applied to Lord Raglan for a commission. Lord Raglan asked him if he knew what had happened to so many of the officers of that Regiment. He replied—" I do, but it is my father's old Regiment." And Lord Raglan was so struck with the courageous but modest bearing of the young lad that he there and then gave him a commission in the 78th. I believe that in General Macpherson's baggage at Ismalia were to be found his summons for firing the cannon on the playground and his first commission by Lord Raglan, tied together. We both knew the same people, and it was interesting to recall old familiar names and personages. Both of us had happy memories of old General William Gordon, of Peninsular fame. I told him the story of how I had been appointed one of a deputation to wait on General Gordon, and ask him, for the satisfaction of the boys of the town, whether he had really shouted out in Gaelic to the Highlanders, "Shoulder to shoulder," and plunged into the water at their head in the famous passage of the Nive. "I did, I did, but it was nothing, my boys; you can all do greater things," said the General, who patted me on the head, and gave me half-a-crown as the spokesman on the occasion. We spent the money in fireworks celebrating the passage of the Nive. General Macpherson appeared amused at my story, and remarked—"But you did not fire any cannon!" "That feat," said I, "was reserved for the Commander-in-Chief of the Indian Contingent!" He laughed good humouredly at the hit at his own youthful escapade.

We had some talk, in which several of the Anglo-Indian officers joined, as to the relative merits of the transport service from England and India, and Sir Herbert (as he afterwards became) appeared anxious to hear my opinion as an outsider. I said there was no comparison. All was in confusion on board the transports from England. The men were in one ship, their ammunition in another, and their stores packed away in some half-a-dozen vessels, whereas in the Indian transports each Regiment carried with it its complete outfit for field service, and could land at any point fully equipped for action at an hour's notice. Within twenty-eight days from the order being received in India, we could have landed 10,000 good soldiers on Egyptian soil, and those that were here were peculiarly fitted by their provident habits, discipline, and adaptability to the climate for the duty on hand. "I quite agree with you," said Sir Herbert.

What a fine sight the Highland Regiments presented as they started for the front. The other regiments were landed helter-skelter on shore, and lay under canvas or trees, but the Highlanders were kept on board ship until wanted for the front, coming ashore merely in companies for fatigue duty. Now they mustered in full force and marched proudly along to the station, the pipes playing "The Campbell's are Coming." The gallant 42nd led the van, with the pioneers with axes in front. The drummer with his tiger's skin on, as if it were midwinter in the far north, beat his drum with great energy, as if he intended each rap for Arabi's head. A few of the soldiers wore the blue veil and goggles, but somehow these things looked a little effeminate with the kilt, and the majority of the men seemed to think so too by not wearing them. There were several companies of cavalry along with the infantry, and General Alison and General Hamley, both one-armed men, if I mistake not, accompanied them. Each man carried two days' rations and 100 rounds of ammunition, which with their rugs, coats, water flask, &c., seemed quite a load. But they marched as steadily and proudly as if on review at Hyde Park. The rear was brought up by the pets of the regiment—two little dogs—a poodle and a Skye terrier, led by a string.

I met Sir Garnet Wolseley frequently. He usually slept on board one of the ships, that is, when he did sleep, for he seemed ever on the move. He is the very ideal of a commanding officer—cool and calm in appearance, but active and determined, and ever on the alert to expedite matters. He has only one eye, but the glass one which serves as a substitute for the lost one appears as if it shone with preternatural intelligence and zeal. He was unstinted in his expressions of commendation of the way in which the Indian troops had been transported, and remarked that it was an object lesson to the War Office authorities at home. I have no doubt the Indian method will in future be adopted throughout the whole transport service. The number of gunboats going ashore through unskilful management was a matter of unfavourable remark.

The conditions of life amidst all the bustle and excitement of landing were very trying. Not a drop of rain had fallen for a month, nor had there been any wind beyond a gentle air in the afternoon since we arrived. These little breezes would be refreshing did they not bring a tainted breath from the ghastly remains they have passed over. The sun is very strong during the day, and the sand retains the heat during the night. There had not been a single degree of difference of temperature throughout the long month; not a cloud visible—the clear silvery sky shining over the white glaring hot sands; there is no sound to break the death-like stillness, save the voices of those who have intruded into the desert. You see ridge after ridge of blown sand reaching to the very edge of the horizon. Occasionally it assumes the most fantastic forms. You perceive something like a broad lake, rippling like a sea, and on its bosom you see ships and steamers, castles, huge forts and armies, when suddenly, as if by enchantment, the scene changes; the lake vanishes, the ships and steamers drop into a huge sand mound, and the men and the castles take the form of spectres and recede into the ghostly distance. It was but a mirage. It was in a scene like this that our British soldiers were encamped waiting for the morrow to begin the attack.

I applied for leave to visit the front, and had taken my seat in one of the Fresh Water Canal boats, but just as we were casting off our moorings we were recalled by an order of the same officer who granted us permission, and instructed to get up steam on board our vessels in case of a surprise. One of our number, however, had got into a steam launch, and was off before the order reached, and found himself at the front the following morning. Finding that he was a sailor and not a soldier, he was supplied with a donkey and ordered to go to the rear. The donkey took charge, and went in the opposite direction, carrying him right into Arabi's camp. His story was that he shook hands with the sentry, and had a drink with Arabi, and started afresh for Ismalia, where he arrived two days after the battle of Tel-el-Kebir had been fought and won!

In anticipation of the result of the battle, we were ordered to Suez, and a few days later got ready to embark natives, invalids and wounded, for Bombay, with a few prisoners for Aden. "Start at once!" was the order. Fires were lighted and steam got up, and we proceeded out of dock and down the Red Sea. How different was the home-coming! The poor fellows were the saddest lot of passengers it had ever been my lot to carry. Although we had a native doctor and an apothecary on board attending them, they died and were buried in the Red Sea at the rate of half-a-dozen per day. When these natives are invalided their case is hopeless. Nothing seems to rally them. They will not, or cannot, eat or drink, and will die rather than take anything outside what their caste permits. A little wine even they will refuse, if offered them in a glass. They are faithful even unto death to their beliefs. Sickness amongst them on board ship is therefore merely a question of how long the body will withstand the disease. The heat in the Red Sea was almost unbearable, as it always is in September, and they had but a poor time of it.

On arriving at Aden, we found a change of plan. Instead of conveying these poor invalids, dropping one here and another there in the ocean, our instructions were to tranship them to a steamer bound for Bombay, and to make preparations for receiving 975 men of the 4th Madras Infantry, who had been belated on their way to the seat of war. A few extra cooking galleys was all we required, for we had been provisioned at the start for four months, as were all the transports of the Indian Contingent. A day or two at Aden sufficed to see us underweigh, and we had an exceedingly pleasant passage across the Arabian Sea. We steamed gaily into

Madras Harbour on a beautiful Sunday morning, the band playing "Johnnie Comes Marching Home." And so ended my experiences in the Egyptian Expedition.

Before leaving, the officers of the Regiment presented me with an address conveying their thanks and best wishes, and along with it a handsome clock and bronzes. Two small gold flags crossed with a wreath of laurel and oak entwined, bore the one the officers' names and the other the terms of the address. Such tokens of goodwill are an encouragement in midst of arduous duty.

On the 8th of September of the following year, I received intimation from the Admiralty that "Her Majesty the Queen having been graciously pleased to approve of the issue of a Medal and Bronze Star to such of her Land and Sea Forces as were employed in the Egyptian Expedition," the Lords of the Admiralty had decided to grant the Medal and Bronze Star to the masters of Transports employed in connection with the operations in Egypt in recognition of the services of these officers in carrying out the transport duties. I accordingly received the Egyptian War Medal.

Although I had not the good luck to have come into close quarters with Arabi Pasha in Egypt, I had the pleasure of shaking hands with him a few months later at the sweet little retreat at Colombo to which he had been taken after the war. He spoke English perfectly. He acknowledged that he was most comfortably provided for, but he longed for liberty and the deliverance of his country. He had a small staff of officers with him, consisting mainly of those who had risked their lives in his cause. His wives, at least a certain number of them, were also with him. He told me that he liked the English very much, but hoped some day, perhaps not far distant, to get justice at their hands. The British Government did not understand the situation. The complications had arisen entirely, he said, through questions of finance, and from his refusing to truckle to the Turk.

Sir Herbert Macpherson I never met again. When he went home, amongst other honours conferred upon him was the freedom of the Burgh of Nairn. I was invited to be present at the banquet given on the occasion, but when I informed the Provost of the town that the date fixed for Sir Herbert's installation as a burgess was the eve of my own wedding I was readily excused. I was at Rangoon a few days after Sir Herbert Macpherson had passed through on his way to Mandalay to suppress a rising of the Burmese, from which expedition he never returned, having died of malarial fever.

Once more I found myself in the Transport Service. We were chartered to carry 650 time-expired men from Bombay to Portsmouth. The housing of the Indian native troops was a comparatively easy matter, but very considerable structural alterations had to be made before the 'tween decks were adapted for the carrying of so large a body of British soldiers. The whole responsibility of making the alterations was thrown upon me. We got on all right and passed inspection, and what was more, had not a single complaint from any one on the passage.

We landed our men at Portsmouth in capital health and spirits. I must say the conduct of these British soldiers was most exemplary. They were ashore, a good many of them, at Malta, but neither there or during the whole voyage did one of them misbehave. Colonel de Vetrie was in command, and amongst the junior officers was Lieut. Mackintosh, a young Inverness-shire laird (Mackintosh of Balnespick). The world is small, and one is always rubbing up against some countryman or other. The officer who superintended our alterations at Bombay had played cricket with me on the Links of Nairn when we were boys!

One of the pleasant incidents of a subsequent trip was a visit we had from General Gordon (afterwards of Khartoum fame) at Suez. He inspected the ship and the troops, and had lunch with us. He impressed me as a very noble fellow. Finding I had been a good deal in China in my younger days, we had a long chat about the Treaty Ports and the ways and customs of the Chinese.

The conclusion I came to from my little experience in the conveyance of troops is that, in the event of a serious war, the steamers of the mercantile marine will be of immense service to the Navy in many ways. Most of the first-class liners can easily be transformed into troop ships. They have good speed, enormous carrying capacity, are easily handled, and could be sufficiently armed for their purpose at very little cost.

CHAPTER IX.

ANIMALS AT SEA.

AMONGST one's shipmates at sea one has to include animals of many sorts, and one gets to know their habits on board ship better even than on shore.

Leaving Calcutta for London on one occasion, we had four elephants on board. It was exceedingly difficult to coax them over the gangway, but this accomplished, our troubles only began. The elephants were securely tied in stalls on the quarter-deck, but ere we had got clear of the Sand Heads they had smashed up the whole fabric, and roamed about the decks loose. They showed abject terror of the sea. They were evidently sea-sick, and nearly broke down our deck houses by pressing against them in their struggle to get away from the sight of the sea, all the time howling frightfully. Night came on, and they were still at liberty. I spent a very anxious time. As soon as day broke, sailor after sailor tried his hand at securing them, but as soon as Jack had given the last professional turn to the cross-lashing, and remarked, "Now then, old boy, that will hold you," the elephant simply relaxed his muscles and the fastenings fell off. We had to give it up and allow them to go about the deck. It happened that we had a couple of stowaway lads on board, and they were told off to act as keepers or herds. In a couple of days these boys and their charges became great friends. The boys were very kind to the elephants, and they in turn showed genuine affection, clumsily manifested no doubt, for their young masters. Each elephant's bill-of-fare was two bundles of hay, two bundles of sugar-cane, and two buckets of water twice-a-day, with a bottle of cold-drawn castor-oil made into a sort of pill with flour and dry-boiled rice. They seemed to enjoy this decoction immensely. During the first few days they wasted a great deal of fresh water by catching bucket after bucket with their trunks and pouring the contents over their backs. This extravagance, however, we put an end to by supplying them with salt water for their bath, but they did not seem to like this, and soon discontinued the practice of washing-down altogether. On getting into fine weather they became very happy and quite domesticated. At meal-times they were invariably to be found waiting at the saloon window for any chance morsel which might be passed out to them. They were not long in discovering that I had absolute power to give or withhold dainties, and long before the voyage was ended they would gather round me when I came on deck and with their trunks imprison me until I sent to the saloon for a supply of sweets. It was quite good-humouredly done —they seemed to relish it as a good joke. Poor fellows, two of them died on the passage, the others we landed at

London for transhipment to the Antwerp Zoological Gardens, where I saw them some weeks later looking miserably ill.

In Bombay one day I was asked if I would take a large case of live snakes. I have to confess—in common, I suppose, with many people—to an instinctive dislike to reptiles. After some consideration, however, regarding the risks to be run, I agreed to call on the proposed shipper of snakes. He informed me that they would be put in a substantial case, and would require no food on the passage, excepting a supply of fresh water daily. He assured me there was no possible danger. "Snakes," he said, "refuse to eat while in captivity, and in the event of any of them dying, a pair of tongs will be supplied you for their removal." Opening a door leading to the compound, he invited me to come and have a look at them for myself. Amidst scores of baskets, I perceived an old Indian, sitting in Eastern style, with a lute or pipe in his hand. "Colo!" shouts the native. I instinctively clutch the door-handle, but he assures me there is no danger, and I am persuaded to remain. The snake-charmer, for such he is, uncovers the baskets one by one, and after playing a few peculiar notes on his lute, a hundred or more hooded cobras sit bolt upright and stare viciously at me. I feel very uneasy, but a few more piping notes from the charmer's lute and they obediently coil themselves away in the same order.

"There now," said my friend the snake-merchant, "what more tractable creatures could you desire on board ship!"

The high rate of freight offered, with no responsibility as to delivering alive or dead, and a guarantee of a case sufficiently strong to hold them—the offer was a tempting one. I consented to take them, and a couple of days later I was afloat in charge of a hundred cobras. For fear of accident, I had the case secured in the extreme after-end of the ship, ready for tilting overboard. Nothing particular happened for some days. A few had died, but they got so mixed up with the live ones, we did not attempt to extricate them.

We tried the snakes with every kind of food, but they refused to eat My chief officer took a very lively interest in their welfare, and more than once suggested to me to have them out for a run—a proposal to which I most decidedly objected. One night I was on the bridge silently admiring the lovely moon lighting up the sea, when I was startled by the chief officer coming up to me and whispering in a low tone, " The snakes are out, sir!" My first question was, " Where are they?" and without waiting for an answer I jumped up on the bridge-rail. I ordered the saloon doors and windows to be instantly closed, and every possible precaution taken to prevent them getting below, but to look for them myself—never! Not so with the chief officer—his wishes seemed now to be gratified, and with a bull's-eye lantern and a large tablecloth he prowled round the deck all night until he had caught the last one of them. From my perch I had various reports from him during the night. One was that a snake had wriggled himself through the bars of a parrot cage, and swallowed the occupants, a couple of beautiful birds I had got in Burmah. We had the snakes confined in beef barrels, and on the strength of the discovery of the food that suited their taste, we put a live chicken into one of the barrels with them. From the knocking and hissing and general turmoil inside, we concluded the chicken had been killed and devoured amongst them, but on opening the lid of the barrel some twenty-four hours later we found the poor chicken was alive—the snakes hadn't ruffled a feather of it. It was plain they would not eat in captivity. The mortality became frightful amongst them as we got into colder weather, and the last snake of the consignment died as we were entering London Docks. The story of the poor little chicken having got abroad, it was exhibited at the Westminster Aquarium as a curiosity!

All animals, I think, suffer more or less at sea. The dreaded sea-sickness is not confined to mankind. Birds even are not unaffected by it. A canary, for instance, droops its feathers with the first roll or pitch of the vessel, remaining downcast for an hour or two, but breaking into song with the first blink of sunshine in smooth water. The pig appears queer and staggery for a bit, but soon gets over its bad fit and quickly reconciles itself to its new surroundings. The pig is the sailor's pet friend. The superstition regarding sailing on a Friday has now pretty well died out, but few sailors would care to kill a pig on Friday. The life on board ship undoubtedly develops intelligence in the pig. A friend of mine had a curious experience of the affectionate attachment of the animal. He had been chief officer of a Glasgow vessel which had been run into by a German steamer in the English Channel. He had been the only one of the deck crew who had been in the vessel on the previous voyage. The pig and he were thus old shipmates. When the collision occurred, the pig followed the mate round the decks, whining like a dog and refusing to part from him for a single moment. To save their lives all on board had to jump into the sea and swim for the shore, to which the vessel had been run. When it came to the mate's turn to jump, the pig came and put its forelegs lovingly round his neck and clung to him as he leapt overboard. In the water it stuck fast to him, and it was with extreme reluctance that the mate, finding himself unable to sustain its weight, shook off the poor animal, and left it to its fate. The mate was rescued, but the poor pig failed to reach the shore.

The rat, which is no greater favourite on board ship than on shore, is clothed in mystery by the sailor's imagination. The presence of rats in a ship is reassuring for the voyage. A rat will not take a passage in a leaky ship if he can help it. I have never known a rat to injure the hull of the ship. If thirsty he will not hesitate to cut a lead water-pipe, but never by any chance will he scratch one having connection with the sea. I have heard this questioned—I am only giving my own experience and observation. They are a great pest on board ship, not only for the food they steal, but also for the articles they appropriate. A cat is of little use among them. Puss is very soon made to feel how helpless she is, and their relations to each other usually end in their becoming fast friends. I have carried traps voyage after voyage without catching a single rat, though the ship was infested by them. The ship-rat appears to know all about these mechanical inventions and carefully avoids them. Once only was I successful. Leaving Port Said bound home on one occasion, the steward put a fresh bunch of lettuce into a trap which had been set a hundred times before, with every conceivable kind of food, to no purpose. Next morning we found the trap literally crammed with rats. The wonder was how so many managed to squeeze into it. Next evening we repeated the lettuce bait, but the charm was gone. The rats were not exterminated, but not one of them would go near it, and the tempting bit of lettuce remained untouched. I remember on one occasion the ship's carpenter coming upon a rat's nest with four young ones—they were probably not more than a day old. With the view of catching the parents we put the nest of young rats into a goodly-sized wire trap, placing it away in a quiet corner. We expected next morning to see the trap sprung, but no—night after night passed, but no capture was made. Meanwhile the young rats grew splendidly and gambolled about like kittens. Somehow or other the parents had devised means of nursing their progeny without endangering their own liberty.

Sheep make good sailors. Their habit of sticking close together probably enables them to acquire sea-legs sooner than other animals. They become quite tame after a short experience on board ship. We are generally supplied with blackfaced sheep leaving England, but as we go Eastward we get sheep of all sorts and conditions. Amongst the lot driven on board at Port Said, we find the long, lean, lanky and horned Egyptian sheep, and the Aden or Cape sheep with tails nearly half the weight of their whole bodies. Curiously enough, our Highland sheep will not associate with the latter—they seem to have nothing in common. And perhaps no wonder, for the resemblance of some of them to the sheep kind is very slight. Instead of wool they are coated with rough hair. The Egyptian sheep are fond of water. I have seen half-a-dozen of them during the hot weather in the Red Sea reaching up to the chart-room window and pawing it until I turned out and gave them a tumbler of water each. Once in Genoa we were supplied with one of the most extraordinary-looking animals of the breed I have ever set eyes on. His horns were twisted nearly twice round, and his nose was a real "Wellington." He was at home on board in a few hours after his arrival, and continued to enlarge the circle of his friends by making some three or four voyages with me to India. In the matter of food he was by no means particular. Pea soup was his favourite dish. Hot potatoes or any vegetable he took a fancy to were easily obtainable. He had but to watch the sailor who carried these things from the galley to the foc'sle, and by butting him until he rolled over or threw the contents of the dish to him he succeeded in getting the desired dainties. He became latterly the terror of the sailors' lives at meal hours, but his outrageous conduct having been the result of their own teaching, they never complained. His evil practices, however, became so great that I had, though with some regret, to close his career as a shipmate.

I remember once picking up a young crow in the River Hooghly. I found him, with a number of his own tribe, darting hither and thither, cawing frantically around the spot. I took him on board, and for several days an army of crows hung about the steamer with, I suppose, the purpose of carrying him away with them should they have a chance, but in this they failed. In a short time our captive developed into a fine grey-hooded specimen, and became quite attached to his new home. He turned out an extraordinary thief. What wasn't given to him he stole, and chuckled with glee when he did a particularly smart thing in that way. A silver spoon or the sailmaker's needle seemed irresistible temptations. He would watch for hours for his opportunity. Bad character as he was, he became a great favourite fore and aft. He made two voyages to India with me, and we became close and intimate friends. Many times at sea and on shore he would get on the wing and take a look around, but always returned before sunset. Passing through the Straits of Messina on one of the loveliest mornings I ever remember, he was sitting on his perch behind me on the bridge, evidently enjoying as much as I did the sight of the beautiful orange groves and the fragrance of their delicious perfume. We had just passed the rocks of Scylla, and were threading our way through the charming scenery of the channel, when my feathered friend could stand it no longer. He gave three ominous croaks, clapped his wings, got underweigh, and steered straight for the shore. He never returned. I felt exceedingly sorry at losing my old shipmate, and somewhat pained that he should have taken so hasty a departure, but his choice of a retreat so charming did credit to his taste.

Coming from Odessa on one occasion, we were passing a little island in the Mediterranean famous as a home of the turtle-dove. It was blowing hard at the time, which I suppose was the reason for two of these beautiful birds taking shelter in our rigging. Early next morning they were on the wing again, but did not proceed far, and returned to the ship, having failed apparently to determine the position of their island home. In consequence of this, they evidently made up their minds to remain quietly where they were and to be as agreeable as possible. They made sweet pets. We touched at Leghorn and Genoa, and finally discharged our cargo at Marseilles, and in three weeks or so were on our passage back to Odessa. The look-out had scarcely reported the little island in sight when these two creatures shot off, like a pair of arrows, towards it, and I saw them no more.

Fogs and strong winds bring many birds to seek an asylum on board ship. On one occasion while on the northern edge of the Tropics, every rope, yard and mast was covered with swallows resting on their way to their destination. The attention of the majority of the birds appeared to be centred on one particular group. I had the curiosity to investigate what was specially interesting about them. I found that they were all more or less maimed or exhausted, and unable to continue their flight. After a few hours' rest they seemed to recover strength, and amid a perfect babel of twittering and chirupping, the whole flock took flight and proceeded on their journey towards the Equator.

In the Gulf of Aden I have seen land winds, accompanied by fog, bringing on board hundreds of pretty birds, sometimes chased by hawks, who actually killed some of them before our eyes. The storm and stress of weather seemed advantageous to the birds of prey to pursue their quarry.

Crossing the Arabian Sea on a voyage to Bombay about the change of the monsoon season, a peculiar-looking black cloud slowly descended until it burst by coming in contact with our masts, and literally covered our decks to a depth of nearly a foot with locusts. The sea for half-a-mile around was black with them. The fish in shoals came to the surface and devoured them greedily. It may appear almost incredible, but it is an actual fact, that all hands were employed for several hours shovelling the locusts off the decks into the sea. I suppose they were lifted off the heated plains in Asia by some storm, carried high up into the sky, and dropped as if from a balloon upon us as we were nearing Bombay.

The dog forms a strong attachment to his ship, and becomes almost like one of the crew. Crossing the Bay of Biscay in very stormy weather, we sighted a boat flying signals of distress. It was rather a difficult job rounding to, but on coming up we found that it was a shipwrecked crew—they had abandoned their ship as a derelict two days before. The captain presented me with his dog, and the creature seemed to understand the nature of the transaction, for it followed me to the bridge or wherever I went, minding nobody else. "Rover" was "the captain's dog," and transferred his allegiance to whoever occupied that position. I had a small Skye terrier, called "Dulsie," for many years. He was a most devoted little creature. He never left me night or day for a single moment on board ship. He was always on the watch to protect me from danger. If a ragged sailor came along, "Dulsie" at once was on his guard, and snapped at the man's heels if he got a chance. On the stormiest nights he was with me on the bridge, whining plaintively when the sea became very rough. When I went below "Dulsie" also retired; when I was on duty on deck, "Dulsie" also kept watch. I took him on shore at Greenock one evening, and in passing through a crowd lost him—I think he must have been stolen.

On board a sailing ship in which I was mate we had a large St. Bernard's dog of preternatural keenness of scent. We often knew of the proximity of land or of a ship before the man on the look-out had sighted the object by the manifestations of "Ralph." On one occasion he was instrumental in saving the lives of five castaways. We were crossing the China Sea, homeward bound, and were thirty or forty miles off the Island of Formosa. The dog began whining and running about, and trying all he could to direct our attention to something to leeward. I took the glass and scanned the horizon, but could perceive nothing. The dog would not keep quiet, and jumping up put his forepaws on the rail and his head low down between his legs, as much as to say, "This is the bearance." I took the hint, and resting the glass on his head scanned the surface of the water in the direction in which he was pointing. Sure enough there was a black object about four miles away. I reported the circumstance to the captain, and sailed towards it. We made out shortly that it was a raft, and when within half-a-mile or so, I lowered the boat, took "Ralph" with us, and rowed for it. We found five Formosa fishermen on it, more dead than alive. They had been driven off the shore by a storm, and had been tossing about on the ocean for several days. Two of their original number had died. The poor fellows were in a terribly exhausted condition. We took them on board the ship, and fed and clothed them. The captain had an interview with their leader or skipper, and was astounded to find that the old chap was a Freemason, much higher up in the craft than he was. Not being up to this time a Masonic brother, I cannot personally vouch for the fact, but I had no reason to doubt the captain's statement. On the discovery of the fact, the captain instructed me to be very kind to them. A few days later we fell in with a vessel bound for China and transferred our castaways to it. The gratitude these men showed was unbounded, throwing themselves down and kissing one's feet. The St. Bernard dog watched over them as if they were children, and appeared very dissatisfied at their being transferred to the other ship.

CHAPTER X.

MORAL IMPROVEMENT OF THE SAILOR.

SUNDAY at Sea! Strangely enough I have to date most of my greatest trials and troubles on the ocean on Sundays, and yet the memory of Sundays at sea comes back upon me as a time of singular peace and happiness. There is a peculiar beauty and simplicity in a religious service on the deck of a ship at sea. Ever since I had command, I have insisted on Sunday being observed on board my ship, as far as possible, by the curtailment of work and by a religious service being held. If we had no parson on board, I conducted the service myself; if we were fortunate in having a clergyman, then I was content to take up the collection. I have heard some shipmasters say that such services tend to relax discipline. I never found it so. On the contrary, I think the existence of a regular Sunday service adds moral weight to the captain's authority, and has a distinctly humanising and otherwise salutary effect on the ship's company. In passenger steamers it is never omitted, and in sailing ships it is common enough to be made universal, if examples were wanted. If the sailors do not come of their own accord, I would not compel or concuss them, but I should certainly not hesitate to require the attendance of officers and apprentices—in fact, all belonging to the after-end of the ship—when not on duty. I, however, never experienced any difficulty in the matter.

Some times a service at sea is subject to curious interruptions. The minister may have to stop in order that the sailors may have a pull on a slack sail, and that they cannot do without at least singing the refrain of a nautical song. I remember a worthy minister conducting service on the main deck the first Sabbath afternoon we were out. The ship began to pitch, and the clergyman was by no means steady on his legs. I was officer of the watch, and looked about me for something to steady the preacher, and my eye lighted on an empty pork barrel. A sailor fetched it along, and waiting until the minister had finished a sentence, I lifted him bodily off the slushy deck into the barrel, which we made fast, and enabled him to finish his discourse with dry feet and some degree of steadiness. By the time next Sunday had come round, the carpenter had rigged up the barrel into a perfect little gem of a pulpit, draped with cloth and book-board in front. During the whole voyage to Australia our chaplain never missed a Sunday service from this little pulpit.

Although a good deal has been done for the moral improvement of the sailor, there is room for much more work in the same direction. At Genoa the sailors' mission has been a conspicuous success, and I have frequently witnessed evidences of the good Mr Miller and his band of workers are doing among seafaring men of all nationalities. At most of the larger ports, Bethels —sailors' chapels—have been established, and it is the common practice in every foreign port where English ships do congregate to hold a service aboard of one of them, and to invite the officers and men of all the others to attend. These services are, as a rule, very bright and happy. To hear, for instance, the Mahommedan sailors singing their evening hymn under the walls of Constantinople, is enough to put one to the blush for the want of manly courage on the part of men belonging to a Christian nation. But in this respect, as in many others, things are improving at sea.

A short time ago in Calcutta all the sailors in port were invited on board the floating chapel to a magic lantern entertainment. The lecture (by apparently a new hand amongst sailors) was illustrated by a ship exposed to great danger, but making for a haven of rest. It was amusing to hear the comments made by the nautical audience. When the operator (a grave, dignified clerical gentleman) showed the ship broaching-to in a heavy gale, he was greeted with such cries as— "Hard up!" "Brail your spanker in!" and "Why don't you let go the anchor?" and other orders to which he was quite unaccustomed and evidently did not relish or understand. Unless a speaker is thoroughly conversant with nautical terms, he ought to avoid using illustrations from the sea in presence of sailors.

I had a very funny experience as a speaker at one of

these meetings. A movement was originated in Calcutta for the purpose of providing ambulance stretchers, or, as they are called in India, "dhoolies," for carrying sick or injured men to the hospital, and a system of flags, lights and foghorns was formed as signals betwixt the ships and the newly-built stations along the river banks. Having had something to do with the movement, I was appointed to explain the signals from the platform of the Bethel ship to a large number of sailors and a good many ladies and gentlemen who had taken an interest in the matter. I announced to the assemblage that the signal would now be given, which was three distinct blasts on the foghorn, to bring in the ambulance. The sailors who had been provided with foghorns started off, but, instead of giving three blasts from one horn as arranged, persisted in playing a variety of tunes for nearly a quarter-of-an-hour, to my utter discomfiture and to the evident distraction of the musical ears of the company. But this was not all. It had been arranged that one of my boys should go into the ambulance and be carried out in presence of the meeting. The ambulance was brought in by four lascars dressed in the uniform of the youthful society. Order having been secured, I proceeded to describe its construction and use. On opening it in order to put the lad in, to my horror I found that it had already an occupant. A drunk sailor who had arrived too late for the meeting, finding the thing at the door, quietly took possession of it, and was fast asleep. Without a moment's hesitation, and without the audience knowing anything about it, I shoved the lad in on top of the sailor, and ordered its immediate removal. The lascars of course thought it was part of the programme, and the audience cheered the prompt removal of the "dhooly."

The Indian sailor is gradually ousting the British tar from ships going to the East. It is in a very large measure Jack's own fault. He *will* get drunk on every occasion. The lascar is a sober man, and is invariably amenable to discipline. The sarang, or headman of the native crew, relieves the captain and officers of all trouble with them. I have had hundreds of crews of them, and I remember only one instance of a drunk lascar. The sarang in horror at the sight said—"He have an evil spirit, sahib!" At the same time, the Indian sailor is in no way fitted to take the place of the British tar in cold and stormy weather. They have no physical endurance, and are sadly lacking in spirit when any serious emergency arises. These native crews are cheaper, but I believe it is more to save constant trouble than to effect economy that so many shipowners employ them on their steamships. I have always had the idea that it would be possible in large shipping companies to train sailors, mates and masters for their own particular service, and if that were done, the lascars could be dispensed with. The spread of temperance amongst the sailors as a class generally would enable them to recover the ground they have lost. That may seem unlikely to happen, but I have known it occur among a similar class. The fishermen with whom I associated in my early life as a sailor were very much addicted to drink; now two-thirds of the men belonging to the same community and engaged in precisely the same occupations, with more money and greater temptations, are and have been for a dozen years or more total abstainers. If we had a class of fairly sober men, I would not complain.

In a steamer one misses the "house" apprentices to be found in a big sailing ship. I always enjoyed the hour in the afternoon instructing the boys in navigation. It kept one's heart young. I invariably had the good fortune to have had a nice set of lads along with me, and never had any trouble with them. I don't think I spared them work, but I always endeavoured to impress them with the idea that while they had to learn to perform the laborious work of a sailor, their ultimate destination was to command others. It is a great matter to teach them that they belong aft. I have never known, in my own experience, but one instance of a lad who was brought up in the "house" fall back to the forecastle. They all graduated mates and captains.

The instance which proved the exception was one of those lamentable cases in which a young life was wrecked by sheer inconsiderateness. It occurred when I was chief officer of an Australian clipper. The captain was a cross-grained old chap, who was never happy except when he was down upon somebody. His son

Andrew was a boy in the ship, and the old man took a special delight in making the lad's life miserable. No doubt, the captain thought it showed his impartiality in dealing out a full measure of stern discipline to his own son, but it was a foolish thing to treat the lad worse than he would have done any one else simply because of relationship, and I used to tell him so. In the lad's case there was no shadow of excuse for any such treatment, for he was the smartest and bravest boy I ever came across at sea. Any father might well have been proud of him. He had a most extraordinary eagerness to do difficult and dangerous things. When any hazardous job had to be done aloft, Andrew when in my watch used to come along and say—" May I go, sir?" He seemed to me to have inherited the blood of some old Viking, and revelled in the excitement of danger. The greater the peril the keener was he to be in to it. Some young fellows might wish to do smart things merely for the purpose of showing off or boasting about it, but Andrew's ambition was to do everything that any man dared do at sea. I made more of a companion of him than I used to do with boys, partly perhaps to make up for his father's unfairness towards him, but mainly, I think, because of his attractive character. He used to drink in my stories of perils at sea, and seemed to long for the storm and the hurricane—for a chance of doing the things I had seen done. We had passengers to Dunedin, and Andrew was the life and soul of the whole ship's company, singing the best song and dancing the smartest breakdown. He was the cheeriest of shipmates, and was a favourite fore and aft—except with his old father. The boy bore with the old man's peevish temper and petty tyranny with the best of good humour. After the passengers left us, the captain took him out of my watch, for no other purpose, I believe, than that he could get at him better in the second mate's. We were going round to load at the Chincha Islands, and when off Cape Horn, that region of perpetual storms, all hands were called up one night to reef sails. I had just got on deck, when I found the old man in a towering rage at the lad, calling him "coward" and "no sailor"—the worst epithets that can be applied to a sailor. From that hour the boy sulked. He completely changed his character. He went through his duties like an automaton. On inquiring into the circumstances of the row, I found that Andrew was not to blame. We had a Welsh boy named Inigo Jones, who was afflicted with asthma, and sometimes got very ill when he went aloft. Andrew having finished his own work, lay along the yard-arm to assist Inigo Jones to make some lashing fast, but it was too late—the sail carried away. Hence the row. I sometimes got Andrew to pull me along in the pinnace in the delightful evenings on the South Pacific coast—a perfect dreamland—where we spent several months. But it was of no use. He never recovered his old spirits. As soon as we arrived home, he ran away from the ship, and the next thing I heard of him was that he had shipped before the mast as a common sailor. A year or so later I met him accidentally on shore. He told me how he had shipped as a quarter-master on board a coasting barque, bound up the Baltic, and how they had loaded timber for Inverness. Everything had gone well until they reached the Moray Firth. They were unable to make Cromarty Roads, and held on in the hope of getting a pilot. They took the South Channel, and were nearly abreast of Fort-George when a squall struck the craft. The captain and mate were disabled by a falling spar, and had to be carried below. The second mate was of no use. The night was black as pitch, and in the narrow passage, with the Whiteness Sands on the one side and the Cromarty cliffs on the other, the ship was in a tight corner. Andrew took charge, and must have handled the ship splendidly, for he put her about, and brought her out to the open, without loss of spar or sail. "I had heard you describe the manœuvre," he said in reply to some praise of mine. "Yes, but that was in mid-ocean with plenty of sea-room." "Well," he said, with some emotion, "I only wished that night that my father had seen me do it. He would never have said again that I was no sailor!" Poor Andrew, that bitter word had poisoned his life and spoiled his career.

Some very unlikely boys are sent to sea who turn out well. In a good many instances their guardians have found them to be unmanageable on shore. It is not often, however, that a type of lad I had once goes to sea. One afternoon two gentlemen, the one young, the other old, were ushered into the cabin. The elder gentleman informed me that his young companion had just arranged with the owners of the ship to become an apprentice with me. I was not a little astonished, as the young fellow was dressed up in the height of fashion —velvet coat, kid gloves, and silver-headed walking cane. "Yes," he said, "and I would be obliged, captain, if you would inform me what outfit I will require to purchase." I replied that that depended upon the quantity of clothes he possessed. He produced a list and read out the inventory of a most ample wardrobe for a fashionable swell of the West End. I suggested a few plain things in addition. "There is just one other question I wished to ask you—may I bring my gun with me?" "Oh, no," I said, "the shooting belongs entirely to the captain!" So we parted for the time. I thought, well now, here is a nice business—to be saddled with a fine young gentleman who will be mightily aggrieved when he finds he has got to scrub decks and do all manner of drudgery on board ship for a bit. I never was more mistaken in my life. He put off his shore ways with his shore suit. He turned out a capital sailor. I never heard a word of complaint from him, and before he was a twelvemonth at sea, he could "boss" any crowd of sailors at their work. He was still the gentleman through it all, but a thoroughly manly fellow who knew that work had to be done—and well done too! I left him behind in the old ship when I was transferred to a new vessel, and heard with regret that when his time was out, he gave up the sea and went out to India as a tea-planter, thereby depriving the mercantile marine of a promising commander.

The boys' house in the big sailing ship is really the nursery for the officers of the whole mercantile marine, ships and steamers alike. In my opinion shipowners do not attach sufficient importance to it as an institution, and the system of premiums in force in some lines bars the way to many a deserving lad who wants to go to sea but cannot afford to pay. A well conducted system of apprenticeship would, I believe, materially tend to improve the whole service of the sea.

CHAPTER XI.

CONCLUSION.

HAVING served at sea for a period of forty-two years, I began to have thoughts of retiring, and in 1885 I finally resolved to come ashore for good. I had been master of sailing vessels for fourteen years and in command of steamships for a dozen years, and never lost a ship. I had minor mishaps no doubt, but I never had a serious accident or lost a life at sea. I had not been very long ashore when I received an appointment from the Home Secretary to act as Nautical Assessor in Board of Trade Investigations throughout the United Kingdom. The appointment did not carry very large remuneration, but it was very gratifying to me, as I was the first Scottish sailor who had up to that time been appointed. The work was very congenial, and I had now the opportunity of investigating the facts and circumstances of many a tale of the sea. The attitude of mind I brought to bear in these cases was that of friendliness to the shipmaster. I never could forget the innumerable perils with which the course of the most careful navigator is constantly beset, and if an error in judgment only had been made I was in favour of acquittal. One thing has struck me as very remarkable. In the hundreds of cases on which I sat, and in as many others which came more or less under my observation, I found very few accidents arising from drink. It was rare indeed that there was even the allegation of it. I believe that the masters and officers navigating our ships, large and small, are as a class as steady a body of men as can be found in any profession in the world. The type of the old hard-drinking skipper has practically become extinct, and our ships are officered by a set of very clever, intelligent and sober fellows, vastly superior in many respects to those in charge when I went first to sea. At the same time I was not long engaged in these investigations when I discovered a very common cause of accident which to me was a very great surprise. I found that when accidents occurred not due to stress of weather or to excusable errors of judgment, they almost invariably arose from over-confidence. The comparative immunity from any mishap which a navigator may for a time enjoy is apt to engender carelessness in the navigation of his ship. Every shipmaster has to be on his guard against this tendency. He omits taking a cast of the lead—he does not think it necessary—and as a result the ship goes on the rocks. He did not take the trouble to verify his position by bearance when he had the opportunity, and before morning his ship is ashore. He goes right through a thick bank of fog in the neighbourhood of land without slowing down his engines, and comes to grief. The most fruitful source of accident is trusting to dead reckoning—a calculation or estimate of what the ship is supposed to have run—good enough as an auxiliary or as a check to other means, but a most untrustworthy method alone. Cases of culpable neglect of the most ordinary and simple precautions are rightly dealt with by suspension of certificate. No man in charge of a ship has any justification for not using constantly every available means for avoiding every possible risk or danger, and if at the end of it all he meets with disaster, a court of inquiry will not deal hardly with him.

In a few cases—I am glad to say they were very few—the suspicion of criminality on the part of the owner in sending his ship away in an untrustworthy condition, or with the evident intention of the vessel being lost, did come in, but the difficulty in such cases was to get legal proof to warrant a conviction. Happily such cases are not of frequent occurrence, and are entirely confined to the class of " tramp " steamer, which cannot be too closely watched.

One cause of disaster I have investigated with intense interest, having many years ago been convinced of its existence—I refer to the rules laid down for averting a collision. My attention was first directed to the subject by having had some unfortunate experience of it. I had in my time three collisions—not of great magnitude as to losses sustained, but at the time startling enough. In two of these cases, an experienced and capable pilot was in charge. In all three the same thing occurred—the ship did not answer her helm when the engines were reversed while the ship was still going ahead at full speed. It happened to me in three different steamers. I spoke to very many steamer captains on the subject, but got no confirmation of my view from any one of them, as far as I recollect. They rather ridiculed the idea, and set it down as a mere fancy at a moment of excitement. So firmly convinced, however, was I that one day in the Bay of Bengal, having an opportunity, I laid down a barrel by way of experiment, and spent an hour or two practising the manœuvre on it. The result of my experiment satisfied me that the peculiarity I had observed in the steering of a screw steamer under the conditions usually attendant on a collision did exist, and was the cause of frequent accidents. The fact that it had not been observed by captains and officers of screw steamers was to be accounted for by the circumstance that the sudden stoppage of the engines and a reversal "full speed astern" is seldom required except in cases of threatened or actual collision or similar casualties. I sometimes took occasion to practise it with a star for an object, and the results were the same. During my experience as a Nautical Assessor, I had further proof of the effects of it. Time and again, the master of the steamer related how he had, on observing the ship in his way, given the orders—"Hard a-port," "Stop her," "Full speed astern," and yet somehow he did not clear, though he expected he would have done so.

In 1893, I resolved to draw public attention to the

matter by reading a paper before the Institution of Engineers and Shipbuilders in Scotland, and at their meeting on 21st November of that year the subject was discussed. The points I submitted were these:—1st. If the helm is put hard a-port on board a screw steamer, with a right-handed propeller, going full speed or nearly full speed ahead, and at the same instant the engines are reversed, her head (provided there are no disturbing influences present) will cant to port instead of to starboard. 2nd. That if the helm is put, or rather allowed to run hard a-starboard, the instant the engines are reversed full speed her head will cant to starboard as on a pivot. 3rd. That if a steamer, with a screw such as I have described, going full steam ahead, has another vessel close to on her starboard bow, and that in trying to clear her the helm is put hard a-starboard and the engines reversed full speed, a collision is almost certain. It follows then, that in the event of a collision being imminent with a vessel on the port bow, the helm should be put hard a-starboard the moment the engines are reversed, and if the vessel or danger to be avoided is on the starboard bow, the helm should be put hard a-port the moment the screw is turned astern. The members of the Institution generally agreed with my views, but it was apparent that most of them had to accept my facts on trust.

And yet it turned out that the point I had been pressing for so many years was not a new thing. At the meeting of the British Association at Bristol in

1875, I found that Professor Osborne Reynolds had brought up the matter, and a Committee consisting of Mr James R. Napier, Sir William Thomson, Mr William Froude (one of the scientific advisers of the Admiralty), and Professor Osborne Reynolds, were appointed to carry out an investigation into the whole subject of the action of the screw on the steering of vessels. That Committee conducted a series of trials with the steam yachts of the Earl of Glasgow and the Duke of Argyll, and a steam hopper barge belonging to the Clyde Navigation Trust, and subsequently with Sir Donald Currie's mail steamer "Melrose," and their report, given in in 1877 to the British Association at its meeting in Glasgow, shows that all that I had been contending for had been proved beyond all doubt. No action whatever had been taken regarding it, and collision after collision has been going on ever since in ignorance of there being any such peculiarity in the steering of screw steamers.

The press gave me valuable assistance in bringing the matter before the public once more, and I am aware that Sir Robert Finlay, Solicitor-General for England, privately drew the attention of the Lords of the Admiralty to the subject. I have subsequently had some communication with Sir George Nares in reference to it, but no action has yet been taken to avert the serious consequences which are constantly taking place in collisions at sea by adherence to a wrong rule of the road in the case of screw steamers.

My last service at sea was on board a lifeboat. I

was at Nairn in the autumn of 1885 spending my holidays. One morning at breakfast I received a note from Mr H. T. Donaldson, the local Secretary of the National Lifeboat Institution, informing me that telegrams had been received from Burghead and Findhorn that a vessel was ashore on the Culbin Sands, and asking that the lifeboat stationed at Nairn might be sent to the scene of the wreck, but the fishermen being away, he (the Secretary) had no crew to man the boat—would I help him in the circumstances? A few minutes later I was at the lifeboat house on the beach, and had donned, for the first time in my life, the cork jacket of the lifeboat man. Mr James C. Crawford, a gentleman resident in the place, joined me in doing likewise. By beating up, we got together a volunteer crew. The coxswain of the boat was available, but not more than two or three had ever been in the boat before—in fact, the majority of the "volunteers" were not sailors. Still they had pluck and hardihood, and were anxious to save life even at the risk of their own. We got the boat launched into the surf, and then our difficulties began. For nearly an hour we laboured at the oar trying to get her off shore out of the broken water. It had been a wild night, a tremendous sea was breaking on the shore, and the storm was still raging. We managed to keep her head to the sea, and eventually got clear. With a low sail, we ran eastwards to where the vessel lay, a distance of seven or eight miles. We found the vessel stranded on a sand bank opposite the Culbin Sands, a tremendous sea breaking over her. The Moray Firth narrows at this point, like the neck of a bottle. The Culbin Sands consist of great mounds of drifted sand, extending over an area of many miles. Beneath them lie buried the mansion of Culbin, the farm houses and cottages, fertile farms and luxuriant gardens—nothing is to be seen but a desert of sand, requiring but very little wind to set it in commotion, like the billowy sea. It was outside this inhospitable region that the ship had been driven ashore. As we got round her, we found that her crew still clung to the rigging, and we made signs to them to be ready. But they would not respond. They took us for a crew of savages bent on plunder, and preferred death by drowning to assassination by the hands of the fierce-looking pirates with red night-caps and jackets made of cork, out in a mysterious-looking craft ! They had never seen a lifeboat before. We were in a dilemma, but the difficulty was overcome by one of our crew, a smart young English sailor, Clarence Howe, volunteering to jump on board the vessel with a line. It was a ticklish business, but Clarence managed it, and succeeded in making the foreigners to understand we were friends who had come to save them. And then we began to take them off the wreck. A far abler pen than mine (that of the late Rev. Dr. M'Leod, Birkenhead) has so vividly described the rescue that I prefer quoting his words. "The heaviest toil of all awaited them when they came to the spot where the wreck was caught. The waves rose high as hills and dashed upon the wreck, and then sucking backwards for many yards, came on again with fiercer blows. The crew in the lifeboat had to catch their chance in the brief moments when the waves were rushing towards the vessel. In those brief moments, bringing their boat near, they saved ten men. A moment only was possible each time. In that moment the lifeboat drew near, a man jumped on board, and one by one, all who were on the wrecked vessel were saved. Only brave men could have done the work; only men with skilful hands and loyal hearts. But now they turn their prow back towards Nairn with their precious load. What a pull that was back over the seven miles—the wind beating fiercely, the waves terrible for size. The brave men never lost heart. On they came, nearer to safety by every stroke of their oars—nearer and nearer still. At last they turned the corner of the Old Bar, and the harbour was in view. There, on the pier and along the shore, great crowds were watching. Although they could not share the brave labour of the lifeboat, they shared the sympathy of the heroic men. And when the lifeboat was sighted coming round the coast a great shout of joy burst from the entire crowd. Louder and louder it rose, as, peering into the distance, the people discovered that there were saved men on board. But when the boat swept into the harbour, and it became known that every man of the wrecked crew had been saved, and when the very men, one by one, rescued from near death, stepped ashore, shouting could no longer express the joy that was felt. Many burst into tears, others seized the strangers and embraced them as if they had been sons and brothers."

One or two little details may be added to this description. On the return journey, several times the lifeboat appeared as if she were going to be swamped. The Norwegian skipper became alarmed, and cried out, "Where is de bucket!" He wanted to bale her out. He saw the water was knee-deep, and the next sea we shipped would fill her. He could not understand how we could laugh at his apprehensions. But his wonder and amazement grew when he saw that when we mounted the next crest of the wave the water we had shipped disappeared through the bottom of the boat! The mechanism of the self-acting valve was entirely new to him.

Our Norwegian friends were very grateful to us. They were a very respectable set of fellows, and nearly all belonged to the same village. The vessel was the barque "Himalaya" of Tvedestrand, of 391 tons, laden with a cargo of timber from Sundswall in Sweden, and was bound for Inverness. She had encountered the full fury of the gale during the night, and at six o'clock in the morning was driven ashore on the sands as described. The vessel became a total wreck, and as an illustration of the character of the place where she had stranded, the hull in the course of a few months disappeared beneath the sand. The official record of the rescue states that the number of men saved was nine—there were ten, but the captain in giving his report forgot to count himself! The National Lifeboat Institution voted us their thanks for our services, and their vellum address was presented to Mr Crawford and myself at a public function by the Lord-Lieutenant of the County. The King of Norway and Sweden also presented us with medals, bearing the legend—"For Ædel Daad"—(For a Brave Deed). I received my medal through the Glasgow Local Marine Board under circumstances of peculiar gratification to me. The Chairman on the occasion was Mr George Smith, of the City Line, whose character is an inspiration to every seafaring man on Clyde, and another member of the Board was Mr James Stobo, my partner in business and one of my dearest friends on earth. By chance, I witnessed the presentation of similar medals to three of my shipmates—Mr Crawford, Clarence Howe, and Adam Piercey. It took place at the close of a concert by the Nairn Rowing Club—a very appropriate connection—and I had the honour and pleasure of replying for the lifeboat crew. The rest of the men received pecuniary rewards.

The little incident led me to take a greater interest in the lifeboat service than I had hitherto done, and when the Lifeboat Saturday Demonstrations came to be organised in Glasgow I gave all the assistance I could. My holiday experience had convinced me of the great and noble service these boats are rendering to the poor sailor in a time of storm, and nothing I have ever been engaged in gave me so much pleasure and satisfaction as the raising of a sum of £3000 in the City of Glasgow for a steam lifeboat by the combined efforts of all classes. The Lifeboat Institution in Glasgow has a very capable representative in Mr William Martin. He is just the sort of man one likes to work with in any big undertaking—enthusiastic, quick to see an advantage, and untiring in his efforts to achieve success. I formed a very high opinion of the management of the Lifeboat Institution, both at headquarters in London and in the provinces. There will always be croakers in the world to find fault with every good work without much reason, but as an independent observer having had a good deal of practical experience of one kind or another, I unhesitatingly state that the Institution is worthy of the fullest confidence and the most generous support of the public. The Royal National Lifeboat Institution needs no testimonial from me or anybody else—its work speaks for itself—but as a volunteer hand in its service both at sea and on shore, I feel bound to acknowledge the noble service it is rendering to the country.

One thing I had omitted to do in pursuing my career as a sailor—I had never taken the "extra-master's" certificate. The opportunity for doing so really never occurred in my busy life. To pass "extra" should be the ambition of every sailor. I had now been on shore for some years, and I knew it would be much more difficult for me to pass than it would have been when I was a younger man, but an occasion happening, I set to work for the examination, and went up—but failed! I had made some clerical blunder in working out a calculation, and was rightly put back. I was not going to give in, however, and I appeared at the next examination and passed all right. The examination for this certificate is now a very stiff one, but it seemed rather absurd that I should have to begin with second mate's work—a requirement totally unnecessary in the case of any master holding all the previous certificates. With this parchment in my possession my professional rank as a sailor could go no higher.

The life of a sailor has many drawbacks, but it has also its compensations. The romantic dreams of youth are soon rudely disturbed, and a lad wakens up to the stern realities of hardship, privation and peril. But after all there is an undoubted charm in the constant change of scene and country—the shifting from one quarter of the globe to another, with its endless diversity of interest and beauty; and the very perils and dangers of the sea, which make a life on the ocean wave so precarious, add when over a zest to the enjoyment of existence with which the landsman is entirely unacquainted. It is a noble profession, with possibilities of position and rewards free to all who can win them.

www.ingramcontent.com/pod-product-compliance
Lightning Source LLC
LaVergne TN
LVHW061215060426
835507LV00016B/1943